EYES WIDE OPEN

HOW GOD'S LOVE SETS YOU FREE TO LOVE WITHOUT LIMITS

BY

TERRENCE D. SIMS

EYES WIDE OPEN

www.usapublishinghub.com

Published by: USA Publishing Hub

Printed In United States of America

TABLE OF CONTENT

FOREWORD

Believers, non-believers, and everyone in between, I need to tell you something that might shake your whole foundation of what you think faith looks like. For too long, we've been told that following God means closing our eyes, shutting our mouths, and just going along with whatever comes our way. We've been taught that submission means surrendering our minds, our questions, and our concerns about justice and righteousness.

But I stopped by to tell you today - that ain't what Jesus did!

When Jesus walked into that garden of Gethsemane, He didn't close His eyes to what was coming. He saw it all - the betrayal, the false accusations, the beating, the cross, the separation from His Father. His eyes were

WIDE open to every bit of suffering that awaited Him. And you know what He did? He chose it anyway.

Not because He was a glutton for punishment. Not because He didn't have options. But because His eyes were wide open to something else too - the love of His Father and the liberation of His people.

This book is about that kind of seeing. That kind of loving. That kind of living with your eyes WIDE open to both the cost and the purpose of following God in a world that desperately needs His love.

I call it "Careful Carelessness" - and before you think I've lost my mind, let me explain. God's careful love for us enables our careless love for others. Because we know God cares for us completely, we can love others unconditionally - without needing to protect ourselves, without needing to control outcomes, without needing to get something back. This is liberation theology at its finest, and practical spirituality at its deepest. [1] This is how we love like Jesus loved - with our eyes WIDE open to both the cost and the glory.

Can I get a witness? Then turn the page, and let's get started.

About the Author

Terrence D. Sims is a dynamic, Spirit-filled Christian who leads with prophetic clarity and a transformational vision that challenges believers to live with their **eyes wide open** to God's radical love and justice.

After accepting his call to ministry in December 2001, Pastor Sims was ordained an Itinerant Deacon in 2005 and elevated to Itinerant Elder in 2014 within the African Methodist Episcopal Church. He earned his Master of Divinity from Central Baptist Theological Seminary in 2023, where he received the Philip Wendell Crannell Award for Excellence in Preaching. He most recently served as pastor of Bethel AME Church of Fontana, where, from August 2021 to September 2025, the church experienced rapid growth both spiritually and numerically. In addition to his pastoral and prophetic gifts, God graced him with an apostolic anointing, which led him to plant his first church, Eyes Wide Open Christian Church, in October 2025.

Mr. Sims brings a unique perspective to Christian theology through his extraordinary dual identity as both spiritual leader and healthcare technology executive. With over 30 years of business leadership experience—including growing companies from $4.5 million to $34 million in revenue and successfully defending a Fortune 500 corporation before federal agencies—he understands both the spiritual and systemic dimensions of oppression that keep God's people in bondage.

His revolutionary concept of "Careful Carelessness" emerged from decades of witnessing how performance-based spirituality mirrors the conditional systems of the corporate world, and how God's unconditional love liberates us to love others without limits. As someone who has navigated both boardrooms and sanctuaries, Pastor Sims brings prophetic insight into how spiritual warfare operates through systemic oppression to keep believers performing rather than authentically being, even in the Church.

Pastor Sims attributes his strategic thinking not to human wisdom, but to divine revelation and the guidance of the Holy Spirit. These supernatural insights, combined with his practical experience in organizational transformation, position him uniquely to address the intersection of spiritual warfare, liberation theology, and authentic Christian discipleship.

Currently serving on multiple advisory boards, including OneStep Digital Physical Therapy (focusing on fall prevention for seniors), TEKCHILLS Foundation (supporting education and clean water initiatives for 25,000+ children in rural Ghana), and the Alliance for Physical Therapy Quality and Innovation, Terrence Sims demonstrates his commitment to justice and healing extending far beyond pulpit proclamation.

In 2023, he was honored with the "Excellence in Spiritual Leadership" award by the Neighbors United Political Action Committee, recognizing his prophetic voice in addressing both spiritual and social justice issues affecting communities of faith.

Pastor Sims is also the Owner of Senior Care Authority - Inland Empire, providing senior care consulting and placement services—a ministry extension of his belief that caring for the vulnerable reflects God's heart for justice and dignity.

His theological approach uniquely bridges liberation theology with spiritual warfare theology, revealing how authentic submission to God becomes the ultimate act of resistance against systems designed to diminish human dignity and divine identity. Through "Eyes WIDE Open," he challenges readers to move beyond blind faith to informed submission, discovering freedom not through religious performance but through radical acceptance of God's careful love.

Terrence and his wife, Jennifer, have been married for over 30 years and continue to discover the transformative power of "Careful Carelessness" in their own journey of faith. They reside in Southern California, where they are actively involved in community development and social justice initiatives.

A portion of proceeds from "Eyes WIDE Open" supports justice ministries and community transformation initiatives, reflecting their shared conviction that theology must always translate into tangible liberation for God's people.

Terrence Sims is available for speaking engagements, church revivals, seminary lectures, and community forums on liberation theology, spiritual warfare, and the intersection of faith and social justice. For booking inquiries and additional resources on living the WIDE open life, visit www.terrencesims.com or email contact@terrencesims.com.

INTRODUCTION

WHEN YOU SEE SOMETHING, SAY SOMETHING

You've heard that phrase before - "When you see something, say something. " It's become part of our culture, a call to speak up when we notice something that needs attention. But long before the Department of Homeland Security made it a slogan, Heaven had a version: "When you see Me, tell them."

That's what Jesus told the disciples after His resurrection. When you see God moving, when you experience His love, when you witness His power - don't keep it to yourself. The Early Church understood this. They saw something - the risen Christ - and they couldn't stop talking about it. Acts 4: 20 records their response to authorities who ordered them to stop preaching: "We cannot help speaking about what we have seen and heard."[2]

But here's the problem: too many of us are walking through life with our eyes closed. We're so focused on getting through our daily routines, managing our problems, protecting our comfort zones, that we're missing what God is doing right in front of us.

Some of you are living with your eyes closed because you're afraid of what you might see. You know there's injustice in the world, suffering in your community, pain in your family, but it feels safer to look away. You think if you don't see it, you won't have to do anything about it.

Others have their eyes closed because religion taught them that faith means blind acceptance. You've been told that questioning is doubting, that wrestling with God shows weak faith, that submission means shutting down your mind.

But what if I told you that God wants your eyes WIDE open? What if real faith isn't about closing your eyes but about seeing clearly - seeing the world's brokenness AND God's redemption, seeing people's pain AND God's purpose, seeing systemic injustice AND divine justice?

The Problem with Blind Faith

Let me be clear about something - when people talk about "blind faith, " they're usually misunderstanding what faith really is. Faith isn't believing without evidence; it's trusting based on evidence. It's not closing your eyes to reality; it's seeing a deeper reality that others might miss.

Think about it: Jesus never asked anyone to close their eyes and just believe. Instead, He said, "Come and see" (John 1: 39). [3] He performed miracles in public. He taught in the open. He invited investigation. Thomas doubted the resurrection, and Jesus didn't rebuke him for wanting to see - He showed him the nail prints in His hands (John 20: 27). [4]

The problem with what many people call "blind faith" is that it's not faith at all - it's denial. It's refusing to see problems because we don't want to deal with them. It's accepting injustice because confronting it would be uncomfortable. It's staying in unhealthy situations because change requires courage.

When Submission Means Resistance

Some of you might be thinking, "But doesn't the Bible tell us to submit to God? Doesn't that mean accepting whatever happens as His will? "

Yes, we're called to submit to God. But submission to God often means resistance to everything that opposes God. When you submit to God's kingdom of justice, you resist human kingdoms of oppression. When you submit to God's way of love, you resist humanity's way of hatred. When you submit to God's truth, you resist the world's lies.

This is what Howard Thurman understood when he wrote "Jesus and the Disinherited. "[5] He showed how Jesus, living under Roman oppression, modeled a way of being that was both deeply submitted to God and actively resistant to injustice. This is what Martin Luther King Jr. meant when he said, "To ignore evil is to become an accomplice to it. "[6]

Careful Carelessness: The Heart of Freedom

The concept of "careful carelessness" might seem like a contradiction, but it's actually the heart of how Jesus lived and loved. God's careful love for us - His detailed, attentive, protective, providing love - enables us to love others carelessly - freely, generously, without counting the cost.

When you know that God has your back, you can stick your neck out for others. When you're secure in God's love, you can risk rejection from people. When you're confident in God's provision, you can be generous even when resources are limited.

This isn't recklessness - it's freedom. It's not irresponsibility - it's liberation. It's what Paul meant when he wrote, "For freedom Christ has set us free" (Galatians 5: 1). [7]

Eyes Wide Open to What?

So what exactly are we supposed to see with our spiritual vision? Let me break it down for you:

See the Image of God in Everyone When your eyes are open, you see that every person - regardless of race, class, gender, orientation, nationality, or any other category - bears the image of God. This transforms how you treat the homeless person on the corner, the immigrant in your community, the person who votes differently than you, even your enemy.

See Systems, Not Just Symptoms Open eyes see not just individual sin but systemic sin. You recognize that poverty isn't just about personal choices but about systems that trap people. You understand that racism isn't just about individual prejudice but about structures that perpetuate inequality. As James Cone powerfully stated, "The gospel is the good news that God has intervened in human affairs in the interest of the oppressed. "[8]

See Potential, Not Just Problems When Jesus looked at Peter, He didn't just see an impulsive fisherman - He saw the rock on which He would build His church. When He looked at the woman at the well, He didn't just see her shame - He saw an evangelist who would bring her whole town to faith. Open eyes see what people can become, not just what they are.

See God's Kingdom Breaking In With clear spiritual vision, you start noticing signs of God's kingdom everywhere - in acts of unexpected kindness, in movements for justice, in moments of reconciliation, in communities coming together. You see that God is at work even in the darkest places.

The Call to Prophetic Vision

When your eyes are wide open and you see what God sees, you can't stay silent. You become prophetic - not in the sense of predicting the future, but in the sense of speaking God's truth to power, calling out injustice, and pointing toward God's alternative vision for the world.

The prophets in Scripture had their eyes wide open. They saw the oppression of the poor, the corruption of leaders, the hypocrisy of religious practice divorced from justice. And they spoke up. Amos cried out, "Let justice roll on like a river, righteousness like a never-failing stream" (Amos 5: 24). [9] Isaiah declared, "Learn to do right; seek justice. Defend the oppressed. Take up the cause of the fatherless; plead the case of the widow" (Isaiah 1: 17). [10]

This is our calling too. When we see injustice, we speak. When we see suffering, we act. When we see systems that crush people, we work for transformation.

My Personal Awakening

Let me tell you about a moment when God opened my eyes. I was ten years old, selected to attend a predominantly white elementary school in Birmingham. My parents were apprehensive - they had lived through the violence of the Civil Rights era. But they let me go, and it changed my life.

I learned to see beyond skin color to the heart underneath. I discovered that children, regardless of race, basically wanted the same things - to be accepted, to belong, to be valued. But I also learned that some adults hadn't developed this kind of vision. Some saw me as a threat, an outsider, someone who didn't belong.

God was teaching me early that His vision transcends human categories. He doesn't see black and white - He sees His children. This formative experience shaped my understanding of what Kelly Brown Douglas calls "stand-your-ground theology" - the divine imperative to affirm the image of God in all people against forces that would deny it. [11]

Living with Eyes Wide Open

But here's what I need you to understand: living with your eyes wide open isn't always comfortable. When you see clearly, you see pain you might rather ignore. You see injustice you feel powerless to change. You see broken relationships you don't know how to fix.

But you also see God working in ways you never imagined. You see resurrection in places that looked like death. You see hope sprouting in the midst of despair. You see love conquering hate.

This is the paradox of the wide-open life: the more clearly you see the world's brokenness, the more clearly you see God's power to heal it. The more aware you become of suffering, the more aware you become of God's presence in the midst of it.

What This Book Will Do

In the chapters ahead, we're going to explore what it means to live with our eyes WIDE open. We'll look at:

- How God's careful love for us enables our careless love for others
- How to see people and situations the way God sees them
- What Jesus knew that enabled Him to love without limits
- How to love when relationships get complicated
- The connection between love and justice
- How to stay strong when life gets hard
- Practical steps for living the WIDE open life

Each chapter will combine solid biblical teaching, insights from liberation theology, practical psychology, and real-life stories to help you not just understand these concepts but live them out.

The CARE Framework

Throughout this book, I'll be introducing you to a simple daily practice I call CARE:

- **C** Connect with God's love for you each morning
- **A** Ask God to show you who needs love today
- **R** Respond to one person with God's unconditional love
- **E** Evaluate how God's care enabled your caregiving

This isn't complicated theology - it's practical spirituality. It's a way to live out the careful carelessness that Jesus modeled.

Your Invitation to Freedom

So I'm inviting you to open your eyes. Wide. To see what God sees. To love like God loves. To live like you really believe that the same God who raised Jesus from the dead is at work in your life and in this world.

This isn't safe. It isn't comfortable. But it's real. It's powerful. And it's what the world desperately needs.

Are you ready to see something? Are you ready to say something? Are you ready to live with your eyes WIDE open?

Then let's begin.

CHAPTER 1

THE LOVE THAT SETS YOU FREE

"We love because he first loved us. " - *1 John 4: 19*[12]

F riends, I need to start this conversation by telling you something that might revolutionize how you think about God's love. Most of us have been taught that God's love is conditional - that He loves us IF we're good enough, IF we pray enough, IF we serve enough, IF we believe the right things.

But what if I told you that God's love for you has absolutely nothing to do with your performance and everything to do with His character?

What if the love that created galaxies, that holds atoms together, that breathes life into dust - what if that love is directed at you, fully and completely, regardless of what you've done or failed to do?

This is what I call God's "careful love" - not careful in the sense of cautious or limited, but careful in the sense of FULL OF CARE. God's love for you is detailed, attentive, thorough, complete. He knows the number of hairs on your head (Luke 12: 7). [13] He collects your tears in a bottle (Psalm 56: 8). [14] He knew you before you were formed in the womb (Jeremiah 1: 5). [15]

The Difference Between Careful and Cautious

When I say God's love is "careful, " I don't mean He's careful about who He loves or how much He loves. I mean His love is FULL OF CARE - attentive to every detail of your life, aware of every need, present in every moment.

Think about a master craftsman working on a piece of fine furniture. He's careful - not because he's hesitant, but because he cares about every detail. Every joint must be perfect. Every surface must be smooth. Every angle must be precise. That's the kind of careful love God has for you.

Dietrich Bonhoeffer understood this when he wrote about "costly grace" - not grace that costs us, but grace that cost God everything. [16] God's careful love led Him to pay the ultimate price for our freedom.

The Foundation of All Freedom

Here's the revolutionary truth: it's only when we truly understand and receive God's careful, unconditional love for us that we become free to love others without conditions, without limits, without fear.

Think about it: if we believe God's love depends on our performance, we'll exhaust ourselves trying to earn it. If we think His love can be lost, we'll live in constant fear. If we imagine His love is limited, we'll burn ourselves out trying to be perfect.

But when we understand that God's love is unconditional, unlimited, and unearned - when we really get that in our hearts and not just our heads - it changes everything.

Consider the woman caught in adultery in John 8. [17] The religious leaders brought her to Jesus, ready to stone her according to the law. They were focused on her failure, her sin, her shame. But Jesus saw something different. He saw a woman who needed love, not condemnation. A woman who needed freedom, not judgment.

When Jesus said, "Let him who is without sin cast the first stone," He wasn't just challenging the accusers. He was demonstrating a different kind of love - a love that sees past the failure to the person underneath, a love that offers grace instead of condemnation, a love that sets people free instead of weighing them down.

The Science of Being Loved

Now, some of you might think this is just feel-good theology, but let me share something with you that shows the practical power of this kind of love. Medical research has consistently shown that people who feel loved and accepted have better physical health, stronger immune systems, and longer life expectancy.

Dr. Dean Ornish, in his groundbreaking work "Love and Survival," documents extensively how our relationships and sense of being loved affect our physical well-being. He writes, "Love and intimacy are at the root of what makes us sick and what makes us well."[18] When we live in fear, anxiety, and self-condemnation, our bodies pay the price. But when we live in the security of God's love, everything changes.

The Stanford Forgiveness Project, led by Dr. Fred Luskin, has found that people who practice forgiveness - both receiving it and giving it - have lower rates of cardiovascular disease, reduced stress hormones, and better overall mental health. [19] As Luskin notes, "Holding onto resentment is like drinking poison and expecting the other person to die."[20]

Acceptance vs. Approval: Understanding the Difference

I need to make an important distinction here, because some people get confused about unconditional love. God's unconditional love doesn't mean He approves of everything we do. Acceptance and approval are not the same thing.

God accepts you completely as you are, but He loves you too much to leave you as you are. His love is transformative, not permissive. It's like a parent who loves their child unconditionally but still corrects dangerous behavior. The correction flows FROM love, not as a condition FOR love.

Henri Nouwen captured this beautifully in "The Return of the Prodigal Son" when he wrote about how the father's love remained constant whether the son was home or in a far country, whether he was obedient or rebellious. [21] The love never changed; only the son's awareness and reception of it changed.

Breaking Free from the Performance Trap

So many of us are caught in what I call the "performance trap" - the belief that our worth is determined by our productivity, our achievements, our ability to meet expectations. This trap is particularly vicious in our culture, where we're constantly measured, evaluated, and compared.

But God's careful love breaks this trap. You are not loved because of what you do; you are loved because of who you are - a child of God, created in His image, precious in His sight.

Parker Palmer writes about this in "Let Your Life Speak, " explaining how our true vocation flows not from external expectations but from our inner truth. [22] When we know we're loved unconditionally, we're free to discover and express our authentic selves.

The Liberation of Being Loved

This is where careful love connects with liberation theology. James Cone argued that God's love has a particular concern for the oppressed, the marginalized, the rejected. [23] Why? Because they know what it's like to be told they're not enough, that they don't measure up, that they're excluded from love and acceptance.

But God's love is radically inclusive. It reaches the prostitute and the Pharisee, the tax collector and the zealot, the insider and the outcast. As Gustavo Gutiérrez writes, liberation begins with the experience of being loved by God despite our unworthiness. [24]

From Careful to Careless

Here's where it gets really interesting. When you KNOW - not just believe, but KNOW in your bones - that God's love for you is careful, complete, and unconditional, something amazing happens: you become free to love others "carelessly."

I don't mean careless in the sense of sloppy or thoughtless. I mean careless in the sense of without anxiety, without self-protection, without counting the cost. You can afford to love generously because you're drawing from an infinite well. You can risk rejection because your acceptance is secure. You can give without receiving because you've already received everything you need.

This is what Paul meant when he wrote, "I have been crucified with Christ and I no longer live, but Christ lives in me" (Galatians 2: 20). [25] When your life is hidden in Christ's love, you're free from the need to protect yourself, promote yourself, or prove yourself.

Practical Steps to Receiving God's Love

So how do we move from knowing about God's love in our heads to experiencing it in our hearts? Here are some practical steps:

1. Scripture Meditation Don't just read verses about God's love - meditate on them. Take Romans 8: 38-39[26] and spend a week sitting with it: "Nothing can separate us from the love of God. " Let it sink deep into your consciousness.

2. Practice Receiving Many of us are better at giving than receiving. Practice receiving compliments without deflecting. Accept help without feeling guilty. Receive God's forgiveness without adding conditions.

3. Challenge Your Inner Critic That voice in your head that says you're not enough? That's not God's voice. God's voice speaks love, acceptance, and truth about your identity as His beloved child. As Richard Rohr teaches, God's first word about you is always "beloved. "[27]

CARE in Action: Daily Love Reception

- **C** Connect with God's love for you each morning
- **A** Ask God to show you who needs love today
- **R** Respond to one person with God's unconditional love
- **E** Evaluate how God's care enabled your caregiving

The Story of Marcus

Let me tell you about Marcus, a young man in our congregation who taught me about the power of being loved. Marcus had been in and out of prison since he was seventeen. Drug charges, theft, violation of probation - his record was long and painful.

When he first came to our church, he sat in the back row, head down, barely making eye contact. He later told me he was waiting for someone to tell him he didn't belong there. But instead, Miss Clara, one of our church mothers, went straight to him after service, wrapped him in a hug, and said, "Welcome home, baby."

Week after week, Marcus experienced unconditional love from our congregation. No one asked about his past. No one treated him differently when they learned about his record. They just loved him.

Slowly, Marcus began to change. Not because anyone demanded it, but because love does that - it transforms. He started arriving early to help set up chairs. He joined the men's Bible study. Eventually, he became one of our most faithful volunteers in our prison ministry.

One day, Marcus said to me, "Pastor, for the first time in my life, I believe God loves me. Not the cleaned-up version of me I was trying to be, but the real me - the messed-up, broken, trying-to-figure-it-out me."

That's when I saw it clearly: God's careful love had set Marcus free to love carelessly. He could now walk into prisons and love men who were where he had been, without judgment, without superiority, without conditions.

Love That Sustains Through Everything

Viktor Frankl, the Holocaust survivor and psychiatrist, wrote in "Man's Search for Meaning" that even in the concentration camps, those who knew they were loved - by God, by family members, by friends - had a much higher survival rate. [28] Love literally kept people alive in the most horrific circumstances.

This is the kind of love God has for you. It's not dependent on your circumstances. It doesn't diminish when you fail. It doesn't increase when you succeed. It simply IS - constant, eternal, unshakeable.

Howard Thurman understood this when he wrote that the love of God is "the most revolutionary force in the world. "[29] Why? Because when people know they're loved unconditionally, they can't be controlled by fear, manipulated by shame, or limited by human categories.

The Daily Reality of Love

Here's how to live in this reality every day:

Morning Declaration Start each day by declaring: "I am loved by God completely and unconditionally. Nothing I do today will make Him love me more. Nothing I do today will make Him love me less. I am secure in His love. "

Midday Check-in In the middle of your day, pause and ask: "Am I operating from love or from fear? Am I trying to earn what I already have? "

Evening Reflection End each day by reflecting: "How did God's love show up in my life today? How did His careful love enable me to love others carelessly? "

The Ripple Effect of Received Love

When you live from this place of being deeply loved, it creates a ripple effect. Your family feels it - they experience a parent, spouse, or child who isn't trying to get love from them but has love to give to them. Your workplace feels it - they encounter someone who isn't driven by insecurity but motivated by security. Your community feels it - they meet someone who isn't hoarding resources but sharing generously.

This is how the kingdom of God advances - not through force or manipulation, but through people who know they're loved loving other people into freedom.

Chapter Summary

Everything else in this book builds on this foundation: You are loved by God with a careful, complete, unconditional love. Until you get this, really get this, you'll keep trying to earn what you already have. But when you receive this love deeply, you become free to love without limits.

Divine Truth Spotlight: The Battle for Your Identity

The enemy's primary strategy against God's love is identity confusion. He whispers: "You're not worthy, " "You must earn love, " "God's disappointed in you. " These aren't random thoughts - they're strategic attacks designed to keep you performing instead of receiving.

When you truly know God's careful love, you become dangerous to hell's agenda. A person secure in divine love can't be controlled by shame, manipulated by fear, or limited by human approval.

Spiritual Weapon: When identity attacks come, declare aloud: "I am loved by God completely and unconditionally. This love is my foundation, and no lie can shake it. "

Victory Reality: Your identity as beloved is settled in heaven. The battle isn't to become loved - it's to live from being loved.

In the next chapter, we'll discover how this foundational love transforms your very perception - how being deeply loved enables you to see as God sees.

Love That Sets You Free

I Confess...

Lord, I confess that I have lived as though Your love must be earned. I have performed, strived, and exhausted myself trying to be good enough to receive what You have already freely given. I confess my fear that if I truly saw myself, I would be unlovable—and my deeper fear that You see me that way too.

But today, I choose to receive Your careful love. I confess my need for You to love me completely, thoroughly, and intentionally—not because of who I am, but because of who You are. I open my heart to the truth that while I was still a sinner, You loved me. I receive Your unconditional love as the foundation of everything I am and everything I will become.

Free me, Lord, from the prison of performance. Set me free to love others carelessly because I am securely held in Your careful love. Let this truth sink into the deepest parts of my being and change everything about how I live, love, and see myself.

In Jesus' name, Amen.

Chapter 2

Seeing What God Sees

"The Lord does not look at the things people look at. People look at the outward appearance, but the Lord looks at the heart." - 1 Samuel 16: 7[30]

Now that you understand how deeply you're loved, something shifts in your vision. You start seeing differently. Not just seeing different things, but seeing the same things through different eyes - God's eyes.

Most of us go through life with what I call "surface vision" - we see what's immediately visible, what's presented to us, what fits our preconceptions. But God has "depth vision" - He sees past the surface to the soul, past the behavior to the brokenness, past the sin to the image of God that still remains.

The Problem with Human Vision

Let me tell you what's wrong with how most of us see. We see through filters - filters of race, class, education, past experience, cultural conditioning. We see people as categories rather than individuals. We see situations as problems rather than opportunities. We see differences as threats rather than gifts.

This limited vision is killing us. It's dividing our churches, destroying our communities, and devastating our relationships. We can't love what we can't truly see, and we can't see truly until we learn to see with God's eyes.

A Divine Revelation About Vision

One morning during my devotions, God showed me something that revolutionized how I understand His vision. Both Moses and Jesus had death warrants on their lives as babies. Pharaoh ordered all Hebrew baby boys killed. [31] Herod ordered all boys two and under in Bethlehem killed. [32]

But here's what hit me: God saw those babies not just as victims of injustice but as deliverers of justice. Where human eyes saw vulnerability, God saw victory. Where human eyes saw weakness, God saw world-changers.

This is how God sees. He doesn't just see what is; He sees what can be. He doesn't just see the problem; He sees the purpose hidden within it.

Learning to See People

When I was ten years old, I was selected to attend a predominantly white elementary school in Birmingham. My parents were apprehensive because they had experienced the violence of the Civil Rights era firsthand. But they allowed me to go, and it changed my life.

I learned to see beyond skin color to the heart underneath. I discovered that children, regardless of race, basically wanted the same things - to be accepted, to belong, to be valued. I made friends across racial lines that lasted for years.

But I also learned that some adults hadn't developed this kind of vision. Some of my white classmates' parents saw me as a threat, an outsider, someone who didn't belong. Some of my black community members saw my participation in that school as a betrayal.

God was teaching me early that His vision transcends human categories. He doesn't see black and white - He sees His children. He doesn't see the divisions we create - He sees the unity He designed.

This is especially important for those of us in the liberation theology tradition. At its best, it calls us to see everyone - even our oppressors - as children of God who need redemption. [33] That doesn't mean we ignore injustice or accept mistreatment. It means we fight systems while loving people.

Seeing the Bigger Picture

Learning to see with God's eyes also means learning to see the bigger picture of what God is doing in and through people's lives. Sometimes what looks like failure is actually preparation. Sometimes what looks like a setback is actually a setup for a comeback.

Consider Joseph in the Old Testament. [34] When his brothers sold him into slavery, they saw him as an arrogant kid who needed to be taken down a notch. When Potiphar's wife falsely accused him, she saw him as an object to be possessed or destroyed. When he was forgotten in prison, the cup-bearer saw him as useful only when convenient.

But God saw something different. He saw a future leader of Egypt. He saw someone being prepared to save nations from famine. He saw someone whose suffering would position him to preserve God's people.

Years later, Joseph could say to his brothers, "You meant it for evil, but God meant it for good. "[35] That's the perspective we gain when we learn to see with God's eyes - we can see redemption in the middle of rejection, purpose in the middle of pain, destiny in the middle of difficulty.

When Seeing Becomes Prophetic

There's a difference between seeing and having prophetic vision. Seeing observes what is. Prophetic vision perceives what could be and should be according to God's purposes.

The prophets in Scripture had this kind of vision. When everyone else saw a shepherd boy, Samuel saw a king in David. [36] When everyone else saw dry bones, Ezekiel saw an army. [37] When everyone else saw a virgin pregnancy as scandal, Mary saw the salvation of the world. [38]

Dr. Martin Luther King Jr. had prophetic vision. When others saw segregation as permanent, he saw a beloved community where people of all races would sit together at the table of brotherhood. [39] That's not optimism - that's seeing with God's eyes.

The Danger of Selective Vision

But here's what we need to be honest about: sometimes we choose not to see. We develop selective vision, seeing only what confirms our biases and blinds us to what challenges them.

The religious leaders in Jesus's day had selective vision. They could see a woman caught in adultery but couldn't see their own adultery of the spirit. [40] They could see Jesus healing on the Sabbath as breaking the law but couldn't see it as fulfilling the law's purpose. [41]

We do the same thing. We see the speck in our brother's eye but miss the plank in our own. [42] We see the sins we don't struggle with clearly but develop blind spots around our own issues.

Bryan Stevenson writes powerfully about this in "Just Mercy, " showing how our criminal justice system sees some people as irredeemable while giving endless second chances to others. [43] It's selective vision based on race, class, and power.

Seeing Through the Eyes of Love

Here's the key: to see as God sees, we must see through the eyes of love. Love doesn't mean ignoring problems or pretending everything is fine. Love sees clearly - both the brokenness AND the beauty, the sin AND the image of God, the failure AND the potential for redemption.

Paul reminds us that "now we see through a glass, darkly; but then face to face" (1 Corinthians 13: 12). [44] The "then" Paul refers to is when we're fully in God's presence. But we can begin to see more clearly now by looking through love.

John Gottman's research on relationships shows that successful couples maintain a 5: 1 ratio of positive to negative interactions. [45] They see five things to appreciate for every one thing to criticize. That's not ignoring problems - it's maintaining perspective.

Practical Exercises for Divine Vision

Let me give you some practical ways to develop God's vision:

1. The Image of God Exercise When you encounter someone who irritates or challenges you, pause and say to yourself: "This person bears the image of God. " Look for evidence of that image - creativity, compassion, humor, resilience.

2. The Story Behind the Story When someone acts in ways you don't understand, ask yourself: "What's the story behind this story? What pain

might be driving this behavior? What fear might be behind this anger? "

3. The Future History Perspective Look at current situations from the perspective of future history. How might God use this difficulty for good? What might He be preparing? What larger purpose might be at work?

4. The Kingdom Lens Ask yourself: "How does this person or situation look from the perspective of God's kingdom? " Not through political, cultural, or personal lenses, but through the lens of God's reign of justice and love.

Seeing Systems, Not Just Individuals

One of the most important vision corrections we need is learning to see systems, not just individuals. This is crucial for understanding justice and liberation.

When we only see individuals, we miss the bigger picture. We see a homeless person and think "personal failure" without seeing the systems that create homelessness - lack of affordable housing, inadequate mental health services, wage stagnation.

Michelle Alexander opened many eyes with "The New Jim Crow, " showing how mass incarceration is not just about individual crimes but about a system designed to create a permanent underclass. [46]

Kelly Brown Douglas helps us see how "stand your ground" laws are not just about self-defense but about whose lives are seen as valuable and whose bodies are seen as threats. [47]

CARE in Action: Vision Development

- **C** Connect with God's love for you each morning

- **A** Ask God to show you who needs love today

- **R** Respond to one person with God's unconditional love

- **E** Evaluate how God's care enabled your caregivingThe Healing Power of Being Seen

---

There's tremendous healing power in being truly seen. Not judged, not categorized, not dismissed, but SEEN - in all our complexity, struggle, and beauty.

Henri Nouwen writes about this in "The Return of the Prodigal Son, " describing how the father SAW his son from a long way off. [48] Before the son could apologize, before he could prove his repentance, before he could earn his way back - he was SEEN and loved.

When we see others this way, we participate in God's healing work. We become instruments of divine recognition, affirming the image of God in people who may have forgotten it's there.

A Story of Transformed Vision

Let me tell you about Sister Margaret, an elderly white woman who joined our predominantly black congregation. She grew up in the Jim Crow South, raised with all the prejudices of that era. But late in life, after her husband died, she felt God calling her to our church.

At first, she was uncomfortable. She sat stiffly, barely making eye contact. But our congregation loved on her consistently. They saw past her discomfort to her grief. They saw past her age to her hunger for community. They saw past her race to her humanity.

Slowly, Sister Margaret's vision changed. She began to see that the young black men she had been taught to fear were somebody's sons, brothers, fathers. She began to see that the struggle for justice wasn't about taking something from her but about extending to others what she had always enjoyed.

Before she passed, Sister Margaret said to me, "Pastor, I spent most of my life seeing through the world's eyes.

I'm grateful God gave me a few years to see through His.
"

That's the power of transformed vision. It's never too late to start seeing differently.

Chapter Summary

We cannot love what we do not truly see. When we see people as God sees them - as beloved children bearing His image, as complex individuals with stories and struggles, as potential vessels of divine purpose - then we can love them with the same careful love God has for us.

Divine Truth Spotlight: The Battle for Clear Vision

The enemy knows that distorted vision leads to distorted living. He works overtime to cloud your spiritual sight with:

- Filters of past hurt that make you see everyone as a potential threat
- Cultural programming that categorizes people by race, class, or status
- Religious blindness that sees rules instead of relationships

When your vision is clear, you become dangerous to the kingdom of darkness. You see through lies, recognize

---

divine opportunities, and spot God's movement in unexpected places.

Spiritual Weapon: When vision becomes clouded, pray: "Lord, anoint my eyes with heavenly eye salve. Let me see what You see, how You see it."

Victory Reality: Your eyes are windows to divine truth. The clearer your vision, the more effective your love.

Now that you understand the secret of Jesus's unlimited authority through submission, you're ready to explore what that authority enables: love without any limits whatsoever.

Seeing What God Sees

I Confess...

Father, I confess that I have judged by outward appearance. I have looked at people and seen only their mistakes, their failures, their flaws. I have looked in the mirror and seen only my inadequacies. I have used my limited, broken vision instead of asking for Your divine sight.

I confess that I have written people off—including myself. I have declared "finished" what You have declared "in progress." I have seen endings where You see beginnings, impossibilities where You see potential, worthlessness where You see infinite value.

Today, I ask You to give me Your eyes. Show me how You see me—beloved, chosen, valuable, full of potential. Help me see others the way You see them—not as they appear, but as they are becoming. Give me prophetic vision to call forth the greatness You have placed in people, to speak life where others speak death, to see hearts when the world sees only surfaces.

Let me break down the walls I've built between myself and others. Help me see past economic status, educational background, past mistakes, and political differences to see Your image bearers who need Your love.

In Jesus' name, Amen.

CHAPTER 3

THE SECRET JESUS KNEW

'M y food is to do the will of him who sent me and to finish his work. " - John 4: 34[49]

I need to share something with you that might challenge everything you've been taught about Jesus's power and authority. We often think Jesus could love without limits because He was God. He had divine power, divine knowledge, divine authority. Of course He could love perfectly - He was perfect!

But what if I told you the secret to Jesus's unlimited love wasn't His divinity but His submission? What if the key to His freedom was His complete surrender to the Father's will?

The Gethsemane Revelation

Let's go back to that night in Gethsemane. Jesus knew exactly what was coming - betrayal, false accusation, torture, crucifixion. In His humanity, He didn't want it. "Father, if you are willing, take this cup from me, " He prayed, sweating drops of blood. [50]

But then came the words that reveal the secret: "Yet not my will, but yours be done. "[51]

This wasn't resignation. This wasn't defeated acceptance. This was active submission to a purpose bigger than personal comfort. Jesus knew that aligning His will with the Father's will was the source of His authority and the secret of His freedom.

Submission as Liberation

I know "submission" is a trigger word for many of us, especially those who've experienced oppression. The word has been weaponized to keep people down, to maintain unjust power structures, to silence dissent.

But the submission Jesus modeled is completely different. It's not submission to human authority or earthly powers. It's submission to divine purpose. And paradoxically, this kind of submission is actually liberation.

Jon Sobrino, in his work on liberation Christology, shows how Jesus's submission to God's will meant resistance to every form of oppression. [52] By submitting to God's kingdom of justice and love, Jesus challenged every earthly kingdom built on injustice and hate.

The Authority of Alignment

Throughout the Gospels, Jesus makes remarkable statements about His relationship with the Father:

"The Son can do nothing by himself; he can do only what he sees his Father doing" (John 5: 19). [53]

"By myself I can do nothing; I judge only as I hear, and my judgment is just, for I seek not to please myself but him who sent me" (John 5: 30). [54]

"The words I say to you I do not speak on my own authority. Rather, it is the Father, living in me, who is doing his work" (John 14: 10). [55]

This sounds like limitation, but it's actually the source of unlimited power. By completely aligning His will with the Father's, Jesus had access to unlimited resources, unlimited wisdom, unlimited love.

Watchman Nee understood this principle when he wrote about spiritual authority flowing from submission. [56] The more submitted we are to God, the more authority we carry in the spiritual realm.

The Freedom of Having Nothing to Protect

Here's what's revolutionary about Jesus's approach: because He was completely submitted to the Father's will, He had nothing to protect. He didn't have to protect His reputation - His identity was secure in the Father. He didn't have to protect His life - His life was in the Father's hands. He didn't have to protect His ministry - the results were the Father's responsibility.

This gave Him incredible freedom. He could eat with tax collectors without worrying about religious leaders' opinions. [57] He could touch lepers without fear of contamination. [58] He could forgive sins without concern for controversy. [59]

When you have nothing to protect, you're free to love without limits.

Distinguishing Submission from Subjugation

Let me make this crystal clear: the submission Jesus modeled is not the subjugation that oppressive systems demand. Subjugation is forced, external, and dehumanizing. Submission to God's will is chosen, internal, and humanizing.

Jesus submitted to suffering for our sake, but He never submitted to sin or injustice. He submitted to the cross, but He resisted the religious system that put Him there. He submitted to death, but He overcame the power of death through resurrection.

Submission and Liberation Theology

This is where submission connects powerfully with liberation theology. True submission to God often requires resistance to human systems that oppose God's will.

When Harriet Tubman led slaves to freedom through the Underground Railroad, she was submitting to God's will for liberation while resisting human systems of oppression.

When Dietrich Bonhoeffer participated in the plot against Hitler, he was submitting to God's justice while resisting human evil. [60]

When Rosa Parks refused to give up her seat, she was submitting to God's vision of human dignity while resisting society's dehumanizing laws.

Submission to God's will doesn't make you passive - it makes you prophetic. It doesn't make you weak - it makes you willing to confront powers and principalities.

Discerning God's Will in Practice

But here's the practical question: how do we know God's will? How do we discern what to submit to?

God's Will Always Aligns with God's Character God's will never contradicts His nature - love, justice, mercy, truth. If something requires you to violate these characteristics, it's not God's will.

God's Will Considers the Common Good God's will isn't just about individual blessing but communal flourishing. As Gustavo Gutiérrez teaches, God has a preferential option for the poor and oppressed. [61]

God's Will Requires Spiritual Discernment This isn't about human logic alone. It requires prayer, fasting, community wisdom, and spiritual sensitivity. The Holy Spirit guides us into all truth. [62]

> ### CARE in Action: Daily Submission
>
> - **C** Connect with God's love for you each morning
>
> - **A** Ask God to show you who needs love today
>
> - **R** Respond to one person with God's unconditional love
>
> - **E** Evaluate how God's care enabled your caregiving The Healing Power of Being Seen

Jesus's Daily Practice

Jesus didn't just submit to God's will for the big moments - the cross, the major decisions. He practiced daily submission. Luke tells us Jesus often withdrew to lonely places and prayed. [63] Mark records that Jesus rose very early, while it was still dark, to pray. [64]

This daily practice of alignment kept Jesus centered in the Father's will. It's like tuning an instrument - you don't tune it once and forget about it. You tune it regularly to maintain perfect pitch.

The Story of Submission and Freedom

Let me tell you about Brother James, a man in our congregation who learned this secret. James was a successful businessman, used to being in control, making decisions, calling the shots. But his marriage was falling apart, his children were distant, and despite his success, he was miserable.

One Sunday, I preached about Jesus in Gethsemane, about the power of "not my will but yours." James heard it as a call to submit his entire life - business, family, everything - to God's will.

It wasn't easy. Submission meant admitting he'd been wrong. It meant apologizing to his wife and children. It meant changing how he did business, turning down profitable deals that violated his conscience.

But here's what happened: as James submitted to God's will, he experienced freedom he'd never known. Free from the pressure to control everything. Free from the fear of failure. Free from the exhausting performance of always being right.

His wife told me, "Pastor, I got a new husband. Not perfect, but free. He loves without keeping score. He gives without expecting return. He serves without needing recognition."

That's the freedom that comes from submission to God's will.

When Submission Requires Courage

Sometimes submission to God's will requires tremendous courage. It might mean:

- Staying in a difficult marriage when culture says leave
- Leaving an abusive situation when religion says stay
- Speaking up for justice when it's safer to stay silent
- Forgiving someone who doesn't deserve it
- Admitting wrong when you could maintain the facade

I think of Daniel in the lion's den. [65] He submitted to God's will by continuing to pray even when it meant death. That's not weakness - that's warrior-level strength.

The Paradox of Power

Here's the beautiful paradox: the more we submit to God's will, the more powerful we become. Not powerful in worldly terms - controlling, dominating, manipulating. But powerful in kingdom terms - loving, serving, transforming.

Paul understood this when he wrote, "When I am weak, then I am strong."[66] His weakness (submission) became the conduit for God's strength.

Chapter Summary

The secret Jesus knew wasn't mysterious or complicated. It was simply this: complete submission to the Father's will gives complete freedom to love without limits. When you know you're doing God's will, you don't need anyone's approval. When you're aligned with divine purpose, you don't fear human opposition.

Divine Truth Spotlight: The Authority of Surrender

The enemy wants you to believe that submission equals weakness, that surrender means defeat. This is one of his greatest lies. In God's kingdom, surrender to divine will is the pathway to supernatural authority.

Satan fears believers who have submitted everything to God because they become unpredictable to his schemes. When you have nothing to lose (because it's all surrendered), you have nothing to fear. When your will is aligned with God's will, you carry His authority.

Spiritual Weapon: When facing major decisions, pray: "Not my will but Yours be done. I submit this situation completely to Your purposes."

Victory Reality: True spiritual authority flows from complete surrender to God's will. The more submitted you are, the more dangerous you become to the kingdom of darkness.

In the next chapter, we're going to explore what this authority enables: love without any limits whatsoever.

The Secret Jesus Knew

I Confess...

Lord Jesus, I confess that I have confused surrender with weakness. I have believed that submission to Your will means losing myself rather than finding myself. I have clutched control with white knuckles, terrified that if I let go, everything will fall apart.

I confess my need to protect my reputation, guard my comfort, and maintain my image. I have chosen self-preservation over sacrificial love. I have said "my will" when You called me to pray "Your will be done."

But I want to know the secret You knew—that complete submission to the Father's will gives complete freedom to live without limits. I confess my desire to live surrendered but not shackled, submitted but not suppressed, obedient but liberated.

Teach me that Your will is not my enemy but my truest freedom. Show me that when I release my grip on my own plans, I can receive something far greater than anything I could design for myself. Let me discover that security in You enables generosity toward others, that divine direction eliminates human anxiety, and that heavenly authority trumps earthly opposition.

"Not my will, but Yours be done."

In Jesus' name, Amen.

Chapter 4

Love Without Limits

"Love your enemies and pray for those who persecute you." - Matthew 5: 44[67]

Now we come to the heart of it all - what does it actually mean to love without limits? Not in theory, not as a nice idea, but in real life with real people who really hurt us, disappoint us, and work against us?

This is where the rubber meets the road. This is where careful carelessness gets tested. This is where we discover whether we really believe what Jesus taught or whether we just like the sound of it.

The Scandal of Unlimited Love

Let's be honest - unlimited love is scandalous. It offends our sense of justice. It violates our boundaries. It challenges our categories of deserving and undeserving.

When Jesus said "love your enemies, " He wasn't speaking in hyperbole. [68] He meant actually love the people who are actively working against you. When He said "seventy times seven" about forgiveness, He wasn't giving a math equation. [69] He was destroying the limits we place on love.

This is what got Jesus killed. Not His miracles, not His teachings about heaven, but His unlimited love that broke every barrier society had constructed.

What Unlimited Love Is NOT

Before we go further, let me clarify what unlimited love is NOT:

It's NOT Enablement Loving without limits doesn't mean enabling destructive behavior. Jesus loved the rich young ruler but let him walk away rather than lower the standard. [70]

It's NOT Absence of Boundaries Unlimited love can have firm boundaries. Jesus loved everyone but didn't trust everyone. John 2: 24 says "Jesus did not entrust himself to them, for he knew all people. "[71]

It's NOT Emotional Dependence This isn't needy love that requires reciprocation. It's mature love that gives without demanding return.

It's NOT Denial of Reality Unlimited love sees clearly - the sin, the brokenness, the potential for harm. It loves anyway, but not blindly.

The Components of Unlimited Love

So what does unlimited love actually look like?

1. Unconditional Positive Regard This term from psychology means seeing the inherent worth in someone regardless of their behavior. It's what God does for us - loves us not because of what we do but because of whose we are.

2. Persistent Commitment Unlimited love doesn't give up when things get hard. It's the father waiting for the prodigal son, scanning the horizon every day. [72]

3. Sacrificial Action Love without limits costs something. It requires giving up comfort, preference, sometimes safety for the sake of another.

4. Redemptive Purpose This love always aims at redemption, restoration, and transformation - not just of individuals but of relationships and systems.

The Science Behind Unlimited Love

Scientists studying the heart have discovered that it has its own nervous system - about 40, 000 neurons that can sense, feel, learn, and remember independently of the brain.

The HeartMath Institute has documented that when we experience love, appreciation, and compassion, our heart rhythms become more coherent, which improves our physical health, mental clarity, and emotional stability. [73]

In other words, loving without limits isn't just good for others - it's good for us. It literally changes our physiology.

Love Without Limits in Family

With Your Spouse Unlimited love means loving the person they are, not the person you thought they'd become. It means forgiving the same issue repeatedly without keeping score. John Gottman's research shows that successful marriages have partners who make "repair attempts" even when hurt. [74]

With Your Children Unlimited love means your love doesn't depend on their performance. Whether they make straight A's or struggle in school, whether they follow your path or forge their own - your love remains constant.

With Your Parents This might be the hardest. Unlimited love means loving parents who weren't perfect, who may have wounded you, who may still not understand you. It doesn't mean pretending the hurt didn't happen, but choosing love despite the hurt.

CARE in Action: Unlimited Love Practice

- **C** Connect with God's love for you each morning

- **A** Ask God to show you who needs love today

- **R** Respond to one person with God's unconditional love

- **E** Evaluate how God's care enabled your caregiving The Healing Power of Being Seen

---

Love Without Limits in Community

With Your Enemies This is the ultimate test. Can you love someone actively working against you? Martin Luther King Jr. demonstrated this, writing: "Darkness cannot drive out darkness; only light can do that. Hate cannot drive out hate; only love can do that. "[75]

I think about the Emanuel Nine in Charleston - how the families forgave Dylann Roof even as he showed no remorse. That's not human love - that's divine love flowing through human vessels.

With the Marginalized Unlimited love crosses every boundary society creates. It loves across racial lines, economic divisions, political parties, sexual orientations, national borders.

James Cone argues that God's love has a particular bias toward the oppressed. [76] Not because God loves them more, but because they need liberation more urgently.

The Story of Radical Forgiveness

Let me tell you about Sister Sarah from our congregation. Her son Michael was killed in a drive-by shooting - innocent bystander, wrong place, wrong time. The shooter was a fifteen-year-old kid named Jamal.

For months, Sister Sarah was consumed with grief and rage. But then she had a dream. She saw Michael telling her, "Mama, that boy needs what I can't give him anymore - someone to believe he can be better."

Sister Sarah started visiting Jamal in juvenile detention. First visit, he wouldn't even look at her. Second visit, he asked why she came. Third visit, he cried.

She became his advocate in court, asking for rehabilitation instead of maximum punishment. She visited him throughout his incarceration. When he got out, she helped him get a job.

Today, Jamal calls her "Mama Sarah. " He's a youth counselor, helping kids avoid the streets. At Michael's grave last year, Jamal said, "I took your son, but you gave me life. "

That's unlimited love. That's what transforms the world.

When Unlimited Love Seems Impossible

There will be times when unlimited love seems impossible. When the hurt is too deep. When the betrayal is too fresh. When the injustice is too great.

In these moments, remember:

- You're not the source of love, just the channel
- God's grace is sufficient for your weakness[77]
- The same Spirit that raised Jesus from the dead lives in you[78]
- Perfect love casts out fear[79]

The Multiplication Effect

Here's what's amazing about unlimited love - it multiplies. When you love someone without limits, it doesn't just change them; it changes everyone who witnesses it.

One act of unlimited love can:

- Inspire others to love more freely
- Break cycles of revenge and retaliation
- Heal generational trauma
- Transform community culture
- Spark movements for justice

Chapter Summary

Unlimited love is the most powerful force in the universe. It's what transformed Saul the persecutor into Paul the apostle. It's what turned the Roman Empire from Christianity's greatest enemy into its vehicle for spread. It continues transforming lives two thousand years later.

Divine Truth Spotlight: The Warfare of Unlimited Love

The enemy's greatest fear is believers who love without limits because unlimited love destroys his primary weapons: division, hatred, unforgiveness, and fear. When you love your enemies, you neutralize hell's strategy. When you forgive the unforgivable, you demonstrate kingdom power.

Satan works overtime to convince you that some people don't deserve love, that some hurts are too deep to forgive, that some enemies are too dangerous to love. These are lies designed to keep you in spiritual bondage.

Spiritual Weapon: When you feel your love becoming limited, declare: "By the power of Christ in me, I choose to love without limits. No person, no hurt, no injustice can stop the flow of God's love through me."

Victory Reality: Your unlimited love is a spiritual weapon that demons cannot withstand. The more freely you love, the more territory you take from darkness.

In the next chapter, we'll address what happens when love gets complicated - because it will.

Love Without Limits

I Confess...

Heavenly Father, I confess that I have placed limits on love. I have created categories of deserving and undeserving, worthy and unworthy. I have given love conditionally, withheld forgiveness strategically, and calculated my generosity carefully.

Conditional Love

I have loved when it was easy, comfortable, and safe—but resisted loving when it cost me something.

Calculated Forgiveness

I have kept score, held grudges, and built walls where You commanded bridges.

Limited Generosity

I have enemies I refuse to pray for, people I refuse to forgive, and situations where I refuse to extend grace.

I confess that unlimited love scandalizes me. It offends my sense of fairness, violates my boundaries, and challenges everything I've believed about justice. I have loved when it was easy, comfortable, and safe—but resisted loving when it cost me something.

I confess that I have enemies I refuse to pray for, people I refuse to forgive, and situations where I refuse to extend grace. I have kept score, held grudges, and built walls where You commanded bridges.

But today, I choose to love as You have loved me—without limits, without conditions, without calculation. I confess my need for Your love to overflow through me in ways that make no human sense. Give me the courage to love people who hurt me, to pray for those who persecute me, and to bless those who curse me.

Let Your careful love for me become careless love through me. Make me dangerously generous, scandalously forgiving, and radically loving—because my security is in You, not in what others give or withhold from me.

In Jesus' name, Amen.

CHAPTER 5

WHEN LOVE GETS COMPLICATED

"If it is possible, as far as it depends on you, live at peace with everyone." - Romans 12: 18[80]

Let's get real for a moment. Everything I've said about unlimited love sounds beautiful in theory, but what about when:

- The person you're trying to love keeps hurting you?
- Your love is being used against you?
- Loving someone means watching them destroy themselves?
- Different people you love are in conflict with each other?

- Love requires you to challenge injustice?

This is where love gets complicated. This is where the rubber meets the road. This is where we need wisdom, boundaries, and sometimes holy confrontation.

The Myth of Easy Love

First, let's destroy the myth that if love is real, it should be easy. That's Hollywood love, not Kingdom love. Real love - unlimited, unconditional, transformational love - is often the hardest thing you'll ever do.

Jesus's love led Him to a cross. Stephen's love for his persecutors was expressed while being stoned to death. [81] Paul's love for the churches led to beatings, imprisonment, and shipwrecks. [82]

If your love hasn't complicated your life, you might want to examine whether you're really loving like Jesus loved.

When Love Requires Boundaries

Here's what many people don't understand: unlimited love doesn't mean unlimited access. You can love someone completely while limiting their access to your life.

Dr. Henry Cloud and Dr. John Townsend, in their groundbreaking work "Boundaries, " explain that boundaries aren't walls to keep love out but doors to let healthy love in. [83] Boundaries protect love from becoming enablement.

I counseled a woman whose adult son was addicted to drugs. She kept giving him money, letting him live at home, cleaning up his messes. She called it love. But it was enabling his destruction.

True love required boundaries:

- No money that could be used for drugs
- No living at home while using
- Yes to paying for treatment
- Yes to emotional support in recovery
- Yes to relationship restoration with accountability

The son accused her of not loving him. But the boundaries WERE love - love that refused to enable death and insisted on life.

When Love Means Confrontation

Sometimes love requires confrontation. Not judgment, not condemnation, but truth spoken in love.

Jesus confronted Peter: "Get behind me, Satan! "[84] Sounds harsh, but it was love preventing Peter from becoming a stumbling block.

Paul confronted Peter about his hypocrisy with Gentiles. [85] Public confrontation of a fellow apostle - but it was love protecting the gospel's integrity.

Nathan confronted David about his sin with Bathsheba. [86] He risked his life to speak truth to power - but it was love seeking restoration.

The Art of Loving Confrontation

How do we confront in love? Here are biblical principles:

1. Check Your Motivation Are you confronting to help or to hurt? To restore or to revenge? To build up or to tear down?

2. Examine Yourself First Jesus said remove the plank from your own eye first. [87] Approach with humility, not superiority.

3. Go Privately First Matthew 18 gives the process: first one-on-one, then with witnesses, then to the community. [88]

4. Speak Truth WITH Love Not truth instead of love. Not love instead of truth. Both together, inseparably intertwined.

CARE in Action: Navigating Complexity

- C Connect with God's love for you each morning

- **A** Ask God to show you who needs love today

- **R** Respond to one person with God's unconditional love

- **E** Evaluate how God's care enabled your caregiving The Healing Power of Being Seen

When Love Is Rejected

Here's one of the hardest complications: what do you do when your love is rejected?

Jesus faced this. He wept over Jerusalem: "How often I have longed to gather your children together, as a hen gathers her chicks under her wings, and you were not willing."[89]

Sometimes people aren't ready for love. Sometimes they're so wounded they interpret love as manipulation. Sometimes they're so committed to their path that love feels like judgment.

When love is rejected:

- Keep the door open for future relationship
- Pray for the person consistently
- Examine whether your love had hidden conditions
- Respect their autonomy while maintaining hope

- Grieve the loss but don't let it close your heart

The Story of Complicated Love

Let me tell you about Deacon Williams and his daughter Maya. Maya came out as lesbian in college, and Deacon Williams, raised in traditional theology, couldn't accept it. He quoted Scripture, withdrew affection, and eventually cut off relationship.

For three years, they didn't speak. But Deacon Williams couldn't escape Jesus's command to love. He struggled, prayed, studied, and finally realized: he could hold his theological convictions while still loving his daughter unconditionally.

He reached out, apologized for the withdrawal of love, and said: "I may not understand everything, but I understand that Jesus commands me to love you without conditions. So that's what I'm going to do."

It's still complicated. They don't agree on everything. But love holds them together while they work through the complications.

That's what love does - it stays in the room when everything else wants to leave.

When Love Requires Letting Go

Sometimes the most loving thing you can do is let go. Not let go of love, but let go of control, expectations, or the relationship's current form.

The prodigal son's father had to let his son go to the far country. [90] He couldn't force him to stay. Love required releasing him to make his own choices, even destructive ones.

This is particularly hard for parents. You want to protect your children from pain, mistakes, and consequences. But love recognizes that some lessons can only be learned through experience.

Letting go doesn't mean not caring. It means:

- Trusting God's love for them more than your own
- Recognizing their autonomy and dignity
- Being ready to welcome them back without "I told you so"
- Praying without ceasing
- Loving from a distance when necessary

Chapter Summary

Love will get complicated. Count on it. But don't let the complications make you retreat to limited, conditional, safe love. The world needs people who will love through the complications - who will maintain boundaries while keeping hearts open, who will confront in love while maintaining relationship.

Divine Truth Spotlight: The Enemy's Strategy Against Complex Love

When love gets complicated, the enemy immediately whispers: "This is too hard, " "You're being taken advantage of, " "You deserve better, " "Some people don't deserve love. " His strategy is to use complexity to convince you to abandon love altogether.

But complications are not God's punishment for loving - they're opportunities for love to prove itself real. The enemy fears believers who love through complexity because they demonstrate God's character in the messiest situations.

Spiritual Weapon: When love becomes complicated, pray: "Lord, give me supernatural wisdom to love well in this complexity. Show me how to be both loving and wise. "

Victory Reality: Your willingness to love through complications advances God's kingdom and defeats the enemy's divide-and-conquer strategies.

In the next chapter, we'll explore how finding freedom in God's will enables us to navigate these complications with grace and power.

When Love Gets Complicated

I Confess...

Lord, I confess that I've wanted love to be simple, but my relationships are complicated. I have loved people who hurt me repeatedly. I have struggled to know when to stay and when to create boundaries. I have confused enabling with loving, codependency with commitment.

I confess my desire for easy answers to hard questions. I have wanted formulas when You offer wisdom, rules when You offer relationship, quick fixes when You offer transformation through the mess.

I acknowledge the complicated relationships in my life right now—I name them silently before God. I confess that I don't always know how to love these people well. I have swung between giving too much and withdrawing completely, between tolerating abuse and abandoning altogether.

Truth
When to confront and when to be silent

Boundaries
When to establish limits and when to tear down walls

Grace
When to offer help and when to allow natural consequences

Teach me that complicated love is still love. Show me how Your love for me navigates all my complications—my contradictions, my failures, my brokenness. Help me love others through their complications with the same patient grace You extend to me.

Give me wisdom to know when to confront and when to be silent, when to establish boundaries and when to tear down walls, when to offer help and when to allow natural consequences. Let me love with both truth and grace, both strength and compassion.

Your love is big enough for all our complications.

In Jesus' name, Amen.s

CHAPTER 6

FINDING FREEDOM IN GOD'S WILL

"For my yoke is easy and my burden is light. " - Matthew 11: 30[91]

I need to share something with you that might sound contradictory at first. The more submitted you are to God's will, the freer you become. The more you surrender your will, the more powerful your love becomes. The more you release control, the more authority you carry.

This is the paradox of the Kingdom: slavery to Christ is perfect freedom.

The Burden of Self-Will

Let me start by telling you about the crushing weight of self-will. When you're trying to control everything, manage every outcome, force your agenda - it's exhausting. You become enslaved to your own plans, trapped by your own expectations, imprisoned by your need for control.

I lived this way for years in ministry. I had vision, plans, strategies. I pushed, manipulated, and maneuvered to make things happen. And you know what? Some things did happen. But I was dying inside - stressed, anxious, angry when things didn't go my way.

Then God broke me. A series of failures, disappointments, and betrayals brought me to my knees. In that broken place, I finally prayed the prayer I'd been avoiding: "Not my will, but Yours be done."

The Liberation of Surrender

What happened next revolutionized my life and ministry. As I surrendered my will to God's, I experienced:

Freedom from Outcomes - I was responsible for obedience, not results. Success was defined by faithfulness, not numbers.

Freedom from People-Pleasing - When you're doing God's will, you don't need everyone's approval. God's approval is enough.

Freedom from Fear - If God wills it, He'll provide for it. If He doesn't will it, I don't want it.

Freedom from Comparison - My assignment isn't your assignment. I'm free to celebrate your success without feeling threatened.

This is what Paul meant when he wrote, "It is for freedom that Christ has set us free."[92]

Practical Discernment of God's Will

But here's the practical question: How do we discern God's will? How do we know what to surrender to?

1. Scripture Saturation God's will never contradicts His Word. Immerse yourself in Scripture until God's thoughts become your thoughts.

2. Spirit Sensitivity Jesus said the Holy Spirit will guide you into all truth. [93] Develop sensitivity to the Spirit's leading through prayer, fasting, and silence.

3. Sanctified Common Sense God gave you a brain. Use it. God often leads through sanctified common sense.

4. Community Confirmation Proverbs says there's safety in many counselors. [94] God often confirms His will through mature believers.

God's Will and Justice

Here's where it gets challenging for some: God's will always includes justice. You cannot separate personal spirituality from social justice and claim to be doing God's will.

Isaiah 58 makes this clear. God rejects religious fasting that ignores injustice and oppression. [95] True spirituality that aligns with God's will includes:

- Loosing the chains of injustice
- Setting the oppressed free
- Sharing food with the hungry
- Providing shelter for the homeless

Liberation theology understands this. Jon Sobrino argues that doing God's will means participating in God's project of liberation. [96]

CARE in Action: Aligning with God's Will

- **C** Connect with God's love for you each morning

- **A** Ask God to show you who needs love today

- **R** Respond to one person with God's unconditional love

- **E** Evaluate how God's care enabled your caregiving The Healing Power of Being Seen

When God's Will Challenges Culture

Finding freedom in God's will often means resistance to cultural values. God's will frequently contradicts:

The Culture of Materialism - God's will prioritizes people over profit, relationships over riches, giving over getting.

The Culture of Individualism - God's will emphasizes community, mutual responsibility, and collective liberation.

The Culture of Violence - God's will pursues peace, reconciliation, and restorative justice rather than retribution.

The Culture of Exclusion - God's will creates inclusive community that welcomes all who bear His image.

The Story of Radical Obedience

Let me tell you about Sister Thompson. She was a successful lawyer, making six figures, living the American dream. But she couldn't shake the feeling that God was calling her to something different.

Through prayer and fasting, she became convinced God was calling her to legal advocacy for the poor. This meant leaving her lucrative practice, taking a massive pay cut, and disappointing family who thought she'd lost her mind.

But here's what happened: as Sister Thompson aligned with God's will, she experienced freedom she'd never known. Free from the golden handcuffs of wealth. Free from the pressure to maintain an image. Free to use her gifts for Kingdom purpose.

Today, she's helped hundreds of families avoid eviction, workers receive fair wages, and immigrants navigate the legal system. She told me, "Pastor, I'm making a third of what I used to make, but I'm three times as alive."

That's the freedom that comes from finding God's will.

When God's Will Isn't Clear

Let's be honest - sometimes God's will isn't crystal clear. You pray, fast, seek counsel, and still feel uncertain. What then?

1. Do What You Know Focus on the clear commands of Scripture. Love God, love people, pursue justice, practice mercy.
2. Take the Next Faithful Step You don't need to see the whole staircase, just the next step. Take it in faith.
3. Hold Plans Loosely Make plans but hold them with open hands. Proverbs 16: 9 - we plan our path, but the Lord directs our steps. [97]
4. Trust the Shepherd Even when you can't trace God's hand, trust His heart. He's a good shepherd who leads His sheep. [98]

Chapter Summary

The ultimate freedom isn't doing whatever you want - that's slavery to impulse and desire. The ultimate freedom is wanting what God wants, willing what God wills, loving what God loves. When God's will becomes your food, your sustenance, your delight, you experience freedom that circumstances can't steal.

Divine Truth Spotlight: The Battle for Surrender

The enemy's primary attack against God's will is the illusion of control. He whispers: "You know better than God, " "You can't trust God with this, " "If you don't control it, it won't happen right. " These lies keep you enslaved to your own limited perspective and strength.

True spiritual warfare often begins with surrender. When you submit to God's will, you access divine resources that overwhelm enemy strategies. A submitted believer is the devil's worst nightmare because they can't be controlled, intimidated, or defeated through normal means.

Spiritual Weapon: When struggling to surrender, declare: "Not my will but Yours be done. I trust Your heart even when I can't see Your hand. "

Victory Reality: Your surrender is not defeat - it's the doorway to supernatural victory and divine authority.

In the next chapter, we're going to explore how this freedom enables us to build others up rather than tear them down.

Finding Freedom in God's Will

I Confess...

Father, I confess my anxiety about Your will. I have treated it like a tightrope I might fall off, a puzzle I might never solve, a test I might fail. I have lived in constant fear that I've missed Your plan, chosen the wrong path, or disappointed You irreparably.

Old Perspective

- A narrow path I might miss
- Restriction and burden
- About my performance
- Hiding from me

New Perspective

- An ocean I can swim in
- Freedom and joy
- About Your character
- Inviting me into relationship

I confess that I have made Your will about my performance instead of Your character. I have believed You were hiding Your will from me rather than inviting me into relationship with You. I have sought Your plan more than I've sought Your presence.

Today, I choose to reframe how I think about Your will. I confess my need to see it not as a narrow path I might miss but as an ocean I can swim in. Not as restriction but as freedom. Not as burden but as joy.

I surrender my need to figure out Your entire plan for my life. Instead, I focus on today—on the obedience You're calling me to right now, in this moment. I release the pressure of perfection and receive the peace of Your guidance.

I trust that Your will is good, pleasing, and perfect. I believe that what You've called me to do, You've equipped me to accomplish. I rest in knowing that

Your plans for me are for good and not for evil, to give me a future and a hope.

Your will is my freedom. Your plan is my peace. Your purpose is my power.

In Jesus' name, Amen.

CHAPTER 7

BUILDING OTHERS UP

"Therefore encourage one another and build each other up, just as in fact you are doing. " - 1 Thessalonians 5: 11[99]

Now that you're walking in the freedom of God's will, you have the capacity to do something revolutionary: build others up instead of tearing them down. This sounds simple, but in a culture built on competition, criticism, and cancellation, it's absolutely radical.

The Demolition Culture

Let's be honest about the world we live in. We're surrounded by a demolition culture that specializes in tearing down:

- Social media thrives on outrage and shaming
- News media profits from conflict and criticism
- Politics operates on demonizing opponents

- Even churches sometimes major in what they're against rather than what they're for

Into this demolition culture, God calls us to be builders. Not just builders of programs or buildings, but builders of people.

The Foundation of Building Others

Before you can build others up, you must understand this fundamental truth: every person you meet is made in the image of God and is someone for whom Christ died. This includes:

- The person who cut you off in traffic
- The family member who betrayed you
- The politician you disagree with
- The neighbor whose lifestyle offends you
- The coworker who got the promotion you deserved

When you see people through this lens, building them up becomes an act of worship.

The Principle of Edification

Paul uses the Greek word "oikodome" - literally meaning "house building" - to describe how we should interact with others. [100] Every interaction should add to their structure, not subtract from it.

This doesn't mean false flattery or avoiding hard truths. It means even correction should strengthen, not weaken. Even confrontation should construct, not demolish.

The Science of Affirmation

Research in psychology confirms what Scripture has always taught. The Pygmalion Effect, documented by Rosenthal and Jacobson, shows that people tend to rise or fall to the level of expectation placed on them. [101]

When you consistently affirm someone's potential, their performance improves. When you consistently criticize, their performance declines. Your words literally shape reality.

Dr. John Gottman's research on relationships found that healthy relationships maintain a 5: 1 ratio of positive to negative interactions. [102] Five affirmations for every criticism. Five encouragements for every correction.

Practical Ways to Build Others Up

1. Speak Life Proverbs 18: 21 says death and life are in the power of the tongue. [103] Choose life:

- Point out strengths, not just weaknesses
- Celebrate progress, not just perfection

- Acknowledge effort, not just achievement
- Affirm identity, not just activity

2. See Potential Look at people not just as they are but as they could become. Jesus did this:

- He saw Peter not as an impulsive fisherman but as the rock[104]
- He saw Matthew not as a corrupt tax collector but as a Gospel writer[105]
- He saw Mary Magdalene not as a demonized woman but as an evangelist[106]

3. Create Opportunities Building others up means creating spaces for them to grow, chances for them to contribute, platforms for them to shine.

CARE in Action: Daily Building

- **C** Connect with God's love for you each morning

- **A** Ask God to show you who needs love today

- **R** Respond to one person with God's unconditional love

- **E** Evaluate how God's care enabled your caregiving The Healing Power of Being Seen

---

The Story of Transformation Through Building

Let me tell you about Jerome. He came to our church straight from prison - tattooed, angry, defensive. Most people saw a threat. But Deacon Johnson saw potential.

Every Sunday, Deacon Johnson would find Jerome: "Good to see you, young man. God's got something special for you. " When Jerome missed church, Deacon Johnson called: "We missed you. You're important to this community. "

When Jerome cursed during testimony, instead of embarrassment, Deacon Johnson said, "That's all right, son. God hears your heart. Keep talking to Him. "

Slowly, Jerome began to change. Not because anyone demanded it, but because someone believed he could. Today, Jerome leads our prison ministry. He tells everyone, "Deacon Johnson loved me into who I was supposed to be. "

That's the power of building others up.

Building vs. Enabling

Building others up doesn't mean ignoring problems or enabling dysfunction. There's a difference:

Building says: "You're better than this behavior" Enabling says: "This behavior is okay"

Building says: "I believe you can change" Enabling says: "You don't need to change"

Building says: "I'll support your growth" Enabling says: "I'll protect you from consequences"

Building Across Difference

One of the most powerful ways to build others is across lines of difference - racial, economic, generational, political.

When you build up someone society says is your enemy, you demonstrate the kingdom of God. When you affirm the dignity of someone your culture devalues, you participate in divine restoration.

The Corporate Dimension of Building

Building others up isn't just individual - it's systemic. We need to build systems that build people:

- Educational systems that develop rather than sort
- Economic systems that empower rather than exploit
- Criminal justice systems that restore rather than destroy

- Healthcare systems that heal rather than bankrupt

When we build just systems, we build up entire communities.

Chapter Summary

The church should be the ultimate construction site - a place where broken people get rebuilt, wounded people get restored, lost people get found. We're called to be builders in a world of demolishers, constructors in a culture of critics.

Divine Truth Spotlight: The Warfare of Words

Your words are spiritual weapons that either build up or tear down. The enemy knows this, which is why he works so hard to get negative, destructive, critical words flowing from your mouth. When you speak death over people, you're doing Satan's work. When you speak life, you're advancing God's kingdom.

Every word you speak either advances the kingdom of light or the kingdom of darkness. There's no neutral territory. The enemy fears believers who understand the creative power of their words and use them consistently to build rather than destroy.

Spiritual Weapon: Before speaking about anyone, ask: "Will these words build up or tear down? Am I about to advance God's kingdom or the enemy's agenda?"

Victory Reality: Your commitment to speak life makes you a co-creator with God in transforming lives and communities.

In the next chapter, we'll explore how this building work connects to justice - how love with legs looks in a world of systemic oppression.

Building Others Up

I Confess...

Lord, I confess that I have participated in a culture of tearing down. I have been quicker to criticize than to encourage, faster to expose weaknesses than to celebrate strengths. I have used my words to demolish rather than construct, to wound rather than heal.

I confess my jealousy when others succeed, my satisfaction when competitors fail, my reluctance to celebrate someone else's victory. I have withheld the encouragement others desperately needed because of my own insecurity.

💬 Recognize the Power

My words have power—to build up or tear down, to give life or speak death, to call forth potential or crush dreams.

⦿ See the Potential

See who needs encouragement today, who needs to hear words of affirmation, who needs speech that makes someone believe in them.

📢 Speak Prophetically

Call forth the greatness You've placed within people; speak life where others speak death, see hearts where the world sees only surfaces.

I acknowledge that my words have power—the power to build up or tear down, to give life or speak death, to call forth potential or crush dreams. I confess that I have not always used this power wisely or lovingly.

Today, I choose to become a builder. I ask You to show me who needs encouragement today, who needs to hear words of affirmation, who needs someone to believe in them when they can't believe in themselves.

Teach me to see the potential in people, to speak prophetically about who they're becoming, to call forth the greatness You've placed within them. Help me celebrate others' successes without diminishing my own, to lift others up without tearing myself down.

Make my words instruments of grace. Let every conversation I have today build someone up rather than tear them down. Transform me from a critic into an encourager, from a demolisher into a constructor.

In Jesus' name, Amen.

CHAPTER 8

JUSTICE FLOWS FROM LOVE

"Let justice roll on like a river, righteousness like a never-failing stream!" - Amos 5: 24[107]

Now we come to something that many Christians want to separate but God has joined together: love and justice. You cannot claim to love God while ignoring injustice. You cannot claim to love people while accepting systems that oppress them.

Justice isn't separate from the gospel - it IS the gospel in action. Justice isn't a political agenda - it's a kingdom imperative. Justice doesn't compete with love - it flows from love.

The Biblical Marriage of Love and Justice

Throughout Scripture, love and justice are married, not divorced. Look at God's self-description in Exodus 34: 6-7: "The Lord, the Lord, the compassionate and gracious God, slow to anger, abounding in love and faithfulness, maintaining love to thousands, and forgiving wickedness, rebellion and sin. Yet he does not leave the guilty unpunished. "[108]

Notice that God's love doesn't negate His justice, and His justice doesn't diminish His love. They flow together like two streams joining to form a mighty river.

The prophets understood this. Isaiah 1: 17 commands, "Learn to do right; seek justice. Defend the oppressed. Take up the cause of the fatherless; plead the case of the widow. "[109] This isn't separate from spirituality - this IS spirituality.

Jesus embodied this perfectly. He didn't just preach about God's love - He confronted systems that prevented people from experiencing that love. He:

- Cleansed the temple that had become a den of robbers[110]
- Challenged religious leaders who "devoured widows' houses"[111]

- Ate with tax collectors and sinners, breaking social barriers[112]
- Healed on the Sabbath, challenging oppressive religious rules[113]
- Elevated women in a patriarchal society[114]
- Touched lepers, breaking purity codes that isolated the suffering[115]

Personal Transformation and Systemic Change

Here's what many Christians miss: personal transformation and systemic change aren't competing agendas - they're complementary strategies in God's kingdom. It's not either/or, it's both/and.

Think about it: if you truly love someone who's addicted to drugs, you'll:

- Minister to them personally (personal transformation)
- AND work to change the systems that trap people in addiction (systemic change)

If you love a single mother struggling in poverty, you'll:

- Help meet her immediate needs (personal love)
- AND advocate for policies that address systemic poverty (structural justice)

Dr. Cornel West puts it powerfully: "Justice is what love looks like in public. "[116] Private love without public justice is incomplete. Public justice without private love is soulless.

The Cost of Prophetic Love

Let me be real with you - when love leads you to confront injustice, it will cost you. Jesus warned us, "Blessed are those who are persecuted because of righteousness" (Matthew 5: 10). [117] When you challenge systems that benefit from oppression, those systems will fight back.

Dr. Martin Luther King Jr. understood this. His love for all people - black and white - led him to challenge systems of segregation and economic exploitation. That love cost him his life, but it also transformed a nation. [118]

Archbishop Oscar Romero understood this. His love for the poor in El Salvador led him to speak against government oppression. He was assassinated while celebrating Mass, but his witness continues to inspire justice movements worldwide.

This is what Jesus meant when He said we must take up our cross and follow Him. [119] The cross wasn't just personal sacrifice - it was the Roman Empire's tool for crushing dissent. When Jesus carried His cross, He was confronting the ultimate systemic evil.

Liberation Theology's Insight

Liberation theology, born from the experience of oppressed communities, offers crucial insight here. As articulated by Gustavo Gutiérrez, Jon Sobrino, and James Cone, it recognizes that:

- God has a preferential option for the poor and oppressed[120]
- Sin is both personal and structural[121]
- Salvation includes liberation from oppressive systems[122]
- The church must be a voice for the voiceless[123]
- Theology must emerge from engagement with suffering[124]

This isn't liberal politics masquerading as theology. This is biblical Christianity taking seriously God's concern for justice throughout Scripture.

Think about Mary's Magnificat in Luke 1: 51-53: "He has brought down rulers from their thrones but has lifted up the humble. He has filled the hungry with good things but has sent the rich away empty. "[125] That's not just spiritual metaphor - that's God's agenda for real social transformation.

Seeing Systemic Sin

When your eyes are WIDE open, you start seeing not just individual sin but systemic sin - the ways our social structures perpetuate injustice. This includes:

- Economic systems that exploit the poor
- Criminal justice systems that discriminate by race and class
- Educational systems that perpetuate inequality
- Healthcare systems that treat health as a commodity
- Immigration systems that dehumanize the vulnerable

These aren't just political issues - they're spiritual issues. They're manifestations of principalities and powers that oppose God's kingdom.

CARE in Action: Justice Implementation

- C   Connect with God's love for you each morning

- A   Ask God to show you who needs love today

- R   Respond to one person with God's unconditional love

- E   Evaluate how God's care enabled your caregiving The Healing Power of Being Seen

---

Practical Justice in Daily Life

So how do we live this out practically? How does love lead to justice in our daily lives?

1. Educate Yourself You can't address what you don't understand. Learn about:

- The history of systemic injustices in your community
- Current policies and their impact on vulnerable populations
- Organizations already working for justice
- The experiences of those different from you

2. Use Your Voice Speak up in:

- Conversations that perpetuate stereotypes
- Church discussions about community engagement
- Public forums about local issues
- Social media platforms
- Voting booths

3. Leverage Your Resources Whatever you have can be used for justice:

- Money to support justice organizations
- Professional skills to serve the marginalized
- Time to volunteer for systemic change

- Connections to open doors for others
- Platform to amplify unheard voices

The Church's Prophetic Role

The church has a unique calling to be a prophetic voice for justice. We're not a political party or a social service agency - we're the body of Christ, called to continue His ministry of liberation.

This means:

- Preaching that addresses systemic sin, not just personal morality
- Ministries that transform communities, not just comfort Christians
- Partnerships that cross racial and economic divides
- Advocacy that gives voice to the voiceless
- Discipleship that produces justice-seekers, not just church-attenders

Too many churches have become comfort stations for the privileged rather than transformation centers for society. We've focused on getting people to heaven while ignoring the hell that many experience on earth.

The Story of Love Leading to Justice

Let me share how love led me into justice work. Early in my ministry, I was focused solely on personal evangelism and spiritual growth. I thought social justice was a distraction from the gospel.

Then I met Marcus, a brilliant young man from our congregation who got caught up in the criminal justice system. A minor drug offense led to a harsh sentence because he couldn't afford good legal representation. I watched as the system crushed not just him but his entire family.

My love for Marcus and his family opened my eyes to systemic injustice. I realized:

- The system treated people differently based on race and class
- Poverty was often criminalized
- Families were destroyed by excessive sentences
- Communities were devastated by mass incarceration

I couldn't just pray for Marcus - I had to act. That led me to:

- Advocate for criminal justice reform
- Start a ministry for returning citizens

- Partner with organizations working for systemic change
- Preach about justice, not just personal morality
- Use my platform to challenge unjust systems

Love made it personal. Personal made it urgent. Urgency led to action. Action led to transformation - both in individual lives and in systems.

Justice and Mercy Meet

Here's the tension we must hold: we pursue justice while extending mercy. We challenge systems while loving individuals caught in those systems. We demand accountability while offering forgiveness.

This is the Jesus way. He confronted the woman's accusers (justice) while forgiving the woman (mercy). [126] He cleansed the temple (justice) while dying for the temple leaders (mercy). [127]

Bryan Stevenson captures this in his phrase "just mercy" - the recognition that justice without mercy becomes vengeance, while mercy without justice enables oppression. [128]

Chapter Summary

Justice is simply love with legs. It's love that doesn't just feel but acts. It's love that doesn't just sympathize but strategizes. It's love that doesn't just comfort but confronts. When you truly love someone, you can't accept systems that crush them.

Divine Truth Spotlight: Spiritual Warfare Through Justice

The enemy has convinced many Christians that pursuing justice is "political" rather than spiritual. This is a demonic deception designed to keep the church ineffective against systemic evil. When you fight for justice, you're engaging principalities and powers, not just human systems.

Every unjust system has spiritual strongholds behind it. The spirit of racism, the spirit of greed, the spirit of oppression - these are real demonic forces that must be confronted through both prayer and action. Justice work IS spiritual warfare.

Spiritual Weapon: When facing systemic injustice, declare: "I come against every principality and power behind this system. In Jesus's name, I bind the spirits of oppression and release the Spirit of liberation."

Victory Reality: Your justice work dismantles the enemy's territorial strongholds and advances God's kingdom on earth as it is in heaven.

In the next chapter, we'll explore how to stay strong when this justice-seeking, love-living journey gets hard - because it will.

Justice Flows from Love

I Confess...

Righteous God, I confess that I have separated love from justice. I have claimed to love people while tolerating systems that oppress them. I have prayed without acting, felt compassion without pursuing change, acknowledged injustice without fighting against it.

I confess my complicity in unjust systems—my silence when I should have spoken, my inaction when I should have moved, my comfort purchased at others' expense. I have benefited from inequality while claiming innocence.

I confess that I have wanted justice without the cost of love, or love without the demands of justice. I have chosen comfort over conviction, safety over solidarity, acceptance over advocacy.

But today, I acknowledge that justice without love becomes vengeance, and love without justice becomes sentimentality. I need both to flow together like the river Amos envisioned— powerful, persistent, purifying.

Open My Eyes: To the injustices in my community, the systems that oppress people I know, the ways I might be complicit.

Give Me Courage: To confront the spirit of racism, greed, and oppression that divides Your children and crushes human dignity.

Equip Me for Battle: For spiritual warfare against principalities and powers that perpetuate injustice in our world.

Open my eyes to the injustices in my community, the systems that oppress people I know, the ways I might be complicit. Show me where You're calling me to act, to speak, to stand, to change.

Give me courage to confront the spirit of racism that divides Your children, the spirit of greed that hoards while others hunger, the spirit of oppression that crushes human dignity. Equip me for spiritual warfare against principalities and powers that perpetuate injustice.

Let my love have legs. Let my faith have feet. Let my prayers have corresponding actions.

In Jesus' name, Amen.

CHAPTER 9

STAYING STRONG IN HARD TIMES

"Consider it pure joy, my brothers and sisters, whenever you face trials of many kinds, because you know that the testing of your faith produces perseverance. " - James 1: 2-3[129]

If you've made it this far in the book and you're actually trying to live this way - loving without limits, pursuing justice, building others up - then you've discovered something: it's hard. Really hard. And sometimes it feels like it's breaking you.

Let me tell you something that might encourage you: the fact that it's hard doesn't mean you're doing it wrong. It might mean you're doing it right.

The Reality of Resistance

When you start living with your eyes WIDE open, loving without limits, and pursuing justice, you will face resistance:

- Spiritual resistance from forces that oppose God's kingdom
- Social resistance from people comfortable with status quo
- Internal resistance from your own flesh that prefers comfort
- Systemic resistance from structures that benefit from injustice

Jesus promised this: "In this world you will have trouble" (John 16: 33). [130] But He followed it with hope: "But take heart! I have overcome the world. "

The Wilderness Experience

Sometimes following God's will leads you into wilderness. Remember, the Spirit LED Jesus into the wilderness to be tempted. [131] The wilderness wasn't a detour from God's will - it was the pathway through it.

Your wilderness might be:

- A marriage that's harder than you expected
- A calling that's costlier than you imagined
- A stand for justice that isolates you
- A season of doubt after deep faith
- A time of poverty after provision

The wilderness isn't punishment - it's preparation. It's where God does His deepest work in us.

Howard Thurman understood this. He wrote about how the experience of suffering and marginalization actually deepens spiritual insight and strengthens prophetic voice. [132]

The Anatomy of Endurance

How do we stay strong when everything in us wants to quit? Let me break down the anatomy of endurance:

1. Deep Roots Jeremiah 17: 7-8 describes the person who trusts in the Lord as a tree planted by water, that sends out its roots by the stream. [133] When drought comes, it doesn't fear because its roots go deep.

Your roots must go deeper than your circumstances. This happens through:

- Consistent time in God's presence
- Regular meditation on Scripture

- Authentic community relationships
- Spiritual disciplines like fasting and solitude

2. Clear Purpose When you know WHY you're enduring, you can endure almost any HOW. Viktor Frankl, a Holocaust survivor, wrote that those who survived the concentration camps were those who had meaning beyond their suffering. [134]

Your purpose must be bigger than your pain:

- You're loving because God first loved you
- You're pursuing justice because God requires it
- You're building others because the kingdom demands it
- You're enduring because eternity depends on it

3. Community Support You cannot stay strong alone. Ecclesiastes 4: 12 says "a cord of three strands is not quickly broken. "[135] You need people who will:

- Pray when you can't
- Believe when you doubt
- Stand when you fall
- Remember when you forget

CARE in Action: Endurance Building

- C   Connect with God's love for you each morning

- A   Ask God to show you who needs love today

- R   Respond to one person with God's unconditional love

- E   Evaluate how God's care enabled your caregiving The Healing Power of Being Seen

The Story of Endurance

Sister Patricia's story always encourages me. She felt called to start an after-school program in our neighborhood's roughest area. Drug dealers on the corner. Gunshots at night. Parents struggling with addiction.

First year: Only three kids came regularly. Funding fell through. Volunteers quit. Her car was vandalized. She wanted to quit every day.

Second year: Eight kids. Still no stable funding. Working two jobs to keep it going. Health problems from stress. Family said she was wasting her life.

Third year: Fifteen kids. Small grant came through. Two volunteers stuck. One of her first kids made honor roll.

Today, ten years later: Over 100 kids in the program. Full funding. Twenty volunteers. College scholarships for graduates. Three of her original kids are now teachers.

Sister Patricia told me, "Pastor, years 1-5 nearly killed me. But every time I wanted to quit, God would show me one child's face and whisper, 'For this one.' That was enough to make it through another day."

That's endurance. Not heroic. Not easy. Just one day at a time, held by grace.

When Doubt Comes

Let's talk about something we don't discuss enough in church: doubt during hard times. Even John the Baptist, who baptized Jesus and saw the Spirit descend like a dove, later sent messengers asking, "Are you the one?"[136]

Doubt doesn't mean you've lost faith. It might mean your faith is growing beyond simple answers to complex trust.

When doubt comes:

- Be honest with God about it
- Stay connected to community even when you don't feel like it
- Keep doing what you know to do

- Remember past faithfulness
- Give yourself grace

The Physical Impact of Spiritual Battles

Let's be real - spiritual battles take physical tolls. When you're fighting injustice, loving difficult people, and staying faithful through trials, your body feels it:

- Exhaustion that sleep doesn't cure
- Tension that massage doesn't release
- Anxiety that prayer doesn't immediately calm
- Depression that worship doesn't instantly lift

This doesn't mean you lack faith. It means you're human. Even Jesus was "overwhelmed with sorrow to the point of death" in Gethsemane. [137]

Care for your body as the temple of the Holy Spirit: [138]

- Get adequate rest
- Eat nourishing food
- Exercise regularly
- Seek medical help when needed
- Take sabbath seriously

Chapter Summary

Staying strong in hard times isn't about being superhuman. It's about being sustained by supernatural power. It's not about having no weakness. It's about God's strength being perfected in your weakness. The hard times aren't obstacles to the abundant life - they're often the pathway to it.

Divine Truth Spotlight: Endurance Under Attack

The enemy's strategy during hard times is to convince you that God has abandoned you, that your calling isn't real, that you should quit. He whispers: "If God really loved you, this wouldn't be happening, " "You're fighting a losing battle, " "Nobody appreciates what you're doing. "

But hard times often signal that you're making spiritual progress. The enemy attacks hardest when you're closest to breakthrough. Your willingness to endure reveals the reality of your faith and threatens demonic strongholds.

Spiritual Weapon: During the darkest moments, declare: "I will not quit. I will not give up. God's strength is perfect in my weakness, and His grace is sufficient for this trial. "

Victory Reality: Every moment you choose to endure rather than quit builds spiritual authority that will serve God's kingdom for generations.

In our final chapter, we'll explore what it means to live the WIDE open life daily.

Staying Strong in Hard Times

I Confess...

Lord, I confess that my faith is weary. The journey of loving without limits, pursuing justice, and living with eyes wide open has taken its toll. I face spiritual resistance, social opposition, internal struggle, and systemic barriers that sometimes feel overwhelming.

I confess my doubt in the wilderness seasons—when following Your will has led not to blessing but to difficulty, not to comfort but to challenge. I have questioned whether I'm doing this right, whether it's worth it, whether You're still with me.

I acknowledge my temptation to quit, to close my eyes again, to choose comfort over calling. I confess my exhaustion, my discouragement, and my fear that I don't have what it takes to keep going.

What I Feel

- Weary from the journey
- Doubt in wilderness seasons
- Temptation to quit
- Exhaustion and discouragement

What I Believe

- You led Jesus into the wilderness
- Difficulty doesn't mean I'm off course
- Hard times don't disqualify me
- Testing produces perseverance

But I also confess my belief that You led Jesus into the wilderness, that difficulty doesn't mean I'm off course, and that hard times don't disqualify me from Your purposes. I choose to consider it joy when I face trials, knowing that the testing of my faith produces perseverance.

Remind me that I'm not alone in this battle. Surround me with prayer partners who will intercede, truth-tellers who will keep me honest, encouragers who will strengthen me, and co-laborers who will work alongside me.

Renew my strength like the eagle's. Let me run and not grow weary, walk and not faint. When I am weak, show Yourself strong in me. Let every hard time become a testimony of Your faithfulness.

In this world I will have trouble, but I take heart: You have overcome the world.

In Jesus' name, Amen.

CHAPTER 10

LIVING THE WIDE OPEN LIFE

"I have come that they may have life, and have it to the full. " - John 10: 10[139]

We've covered a lot of ground together. We've explored God's careful love, unlimited forgiveness, the pursuit of justice, and endurance through trials. Now it's time to put it all together into a way of life - the WIDE open life.

WIDE isn't just an acronym - it's a description of how God wants us to live:

Willing to see what God sees Intentional about loving without limits Determined to pursue justice Enduring in faith through all circumstances

What the WIDE Open Life Looks Like

Living WIDE open means:

- Your heart is wide open to God's love
- Your eyes are wide open to reality
- Your hands are wide open to give and receive
- Your life is wide open to God's purposes

This isn't a life of naive optimism. It's a life of informed hope. You see the world's brokenness clearly, but you also see God's redemptive power working.

The Daily CARE Practice

Remember the CARE framework I introduced? Let me expand it for daily living:

Morning - CONNECT with God's Love Before you check your phone, check in with God:

- Receive His love afresh
- Remember your identity as His beloved
- Recall His faithfulness yesterday
- Request His presence today

Midday - ASK God to Show You In the middle of your day, pause and ask:

- Who needs love right now?
- What injustice needs addressing?
- Where is God already working?
- How can I join Him?

Afternoon - RESPOND with Action Take at least one concrete action:

- Encourage someone specific
- Address an injustice you see
- Build someone up
- Choose love over self-protection

Evening - EVALUATE with Gratitude Before bed, reflect:

- How did God's care enable my caregiving?
- What did I learn today?
- Where did I see God working?
- What am I grateful for?

The WIDE Open Life in Relationships

In Marriage WIDE open marriage means:

- Seeing your spouse as God sees them
- Loving without keeping score
- Addressing issues with truth and grace

- Enduring through seasons of difficulty

In Parenting WIDE open parenting means:

- Seeing your children's potential, not just problems
- Loving them toward who they're becoming
- Fighting for justice they'll inherit
- Modeling endurance through struggles

In Community WIDE open community means:

- Seeing Christ in every person
- Loving across all boundaries
- Working for communal transformation
- Building beloved community together

CARE in Action: Total Life Integration

- C Connect with God's love for you each morning

- A Ask God to show you who needs love today

- R Respond to one person with God's unconditional love

- E Evaluate how God's care enabled your caregiving The Healing Power of Being Seen

---

The WIDE Open Life at Work

Your workplace is a mission field for WIDE open living:

- See colleagues as humans, not resources
- Love even difficult supervisors and competitors
- Advocate for fair treatment and just policies
- Endure with integrity when work is hard

This doesn't mean being a doormat. It means being salt and light, bringing kingdom values into secular spaces.

The Story of WIDE Open Transformation

Let me tell you about the Johnson family. Five years ago, they were typical middle-class Christians - church on Sunday, prayers at meals, basically good people. Then they encountered this message of WIDE open living.

They started with small changes:

- Morning family prayers focused on receiving God's love
- Weekly family meetings to discuss who needs love
- Monthly justice projects as a family
- Celebrating endurance through difficulties

Year one was awkward. Year two brought resistance from extended family. Year three saw breakthrough:

- Their teenage son started a justice club at school
- Their daughter began tutoring kids in low-income neighborhoods
- Dad used his business connections for job creation in marginalized communities
- Mom became an advocate for restorative justice

Today, their home is a hub of kingdom activity. Not perfect, but purposeful. Not easy, but meaningful. They told me, "Pastor, we're more tired but more alive than we've ever been."

Breaking Through to WIDE Open

How do we break through obstacles to WIDE open living?

Replace Fear with Love 1 John 4: 18 - Perfect love casts out fear. [140] The more secure you are in God's love, the less fear controls you.

Choose Discomfort 2 Timothy 1: 7 - God hasn't given us a spirit of fear, but of power, love, and sound mind. [141] Sometimes you have to do it afraid and discover courage on the other side.

Create Counter-Culture Romans 12: 2 - Don't conform to this world's pattern. [142] Surround yourself with people living WIDE open. Create communities of courage.

The Multiplication Effect

When you live WIDE open, it multiplies:

- Your openness opens others
- Your love liberates others to love
- Your justice-seeking inspires justice-seekers
- Your endurance encourages endurers

One WIDE open life can transform a family. One WIDE open family can transform a community. One WIDE open community can transform a city.

Making the Decision

So here's the decision before you: Will you live WIDE open?

Will you let God's love open your eyes to see clearly? Will you let that vision lead to unlimited love? Will you let that love lead to persistent justice? Will you endure when it gets hard?

This isn't a one-time decision. It's a daily choice. Some days you'll live it fully. Other days you'll barely crack open. But every day you try is a day you're growing.

The Promise of WIDE Open Living

Jesus promised abundant life. [143] This is it - life WIDE open to God's love, purposes, and power. It's not easy life, but it's full life. It's not comfortable life, but it's meaningful life. It's not safe life, but it's significant life.

When you live WIDE open:

- You experience God's presence more fully
- You see His kingdom breaking in
- You participate in eternal purposes
- You taste heaven on earth

Chapter Summary

The door is WIDE open. The invitation is extended. The resources are available. Your family needs you to live this way. Your community needs you to live this way. The world needs you to live this way. God is calling you to live this way.

Divine Truth Spotlight: The Ultimate Victory

Living WIDE open is the ultimate victory over Satan's kingdom. When you live with eyes wide open to God's love, heart wide open to others' needs, and hands wide open to serve, you become everything the enemy fears: a free, powerful, loving, justice-seeking follower of Jesus.

The enemy's entire strategy depends on keeping you small, fearful, closed, and ineffective. The WIDE open life destroys every chain he's tried to bind you with and demonstrates the reality of God's kingdom to a watching world.

Spiritual Weapon: Declare daily: "I live WIDE open to God's love and purposes. No weapon formed against this calling shall prosper."

Victory Reality: Your WIDE open life is a daily declaration of victory over the kingdom of darkness and a powerful testimony to the reality of God's transforming love.

Living the WIDE Open Life

I Confess...

Father, I confess my desire to live the WIDE open life—eyes open to Your love, others' needs, and the call to justice. I confess that this is both my deepest longing and my greatest fear.

I confess that simplicity on the other side of complexity is what I've been searching for all along: Love God. Love people. Do it without limits. Do it with actions. Do it until I die. That's it. That's everything.

⚒ **Connect:** With Your love every morning

? **Ask:** You to show me needs throughout the day

↻ **Respond:** With careful carelessness

☾ **Evaluate:** Your work each night

I commit to making the CARE framework my daily rhythm—connecting with Your love every morning, asking You to show me needs throughout the day, responding with careful carelessness, and evaluating Your work each night.

I confess my need to choose my battles wisely, to build my support system intentionally, to maintain my connection to You consistently, and to celebrate even small victories gratefully.

I acknowledge that the WIDE open life isn't loud or flashy—it's a quiet revolution of one act of kindness at a time, one forgiven offense at a time, one justice action at a time, one faithful day at a time.

I confess my fear of what this will cost me and my faith in what You will do through me. I surrender my need for spectacular and embrace Your call to faithful. I release my demand for applause and receive Your promise of "well done."

Today, I choose to live with eyes WIDE open— seeing You clearly, seeing others compassionately, seeing injustice courageously, and seeing my own limitations honestly.

Make me a WIDE open person. Transform my life into a testimony of Your love without limits.

In Jesus' name, Amen.

CONCLUSION

SAY LESS, LOVE MORE

"Dear children, let us not love with words or speech but with actions and in truth. " - 1 John 3: 18[144]

We've talked a lot in this book. We've explored theology, psychology, and practicality. We've examined Scripture, shared stories, and outlined strategies. But now it's time for the bottom line: Say less, love more.

The Danger of Words Without Action

The church has become masterful at talking about love. We preach it, sing it, study it, debate it. But Jesus isn't impressed with our vocabulary. He's looking for our love to have legs.

James warns us about being hearers of the word only, deceiving ourselves. [145] It's possible to know everything about love and not actually love. It's possible to have perfect theology and imperfect practice.

The Power of Enacted Love

When love moves from words to action, everything changes:

- Hungry people get fed
- Homeless people get sheltered
- Lonely people get visited
- Oppressed people get liberated
- Broken people get restored

This is the love that transformed the Roman Empire. Not eloquent sermons but enacted service. Not theological debates but transformational deeds.

My Personal Commitment

As I close this book, let me make a personal commitment to you and to God: I'm going to say less and love more. I'm going to:

- Spend less time crafting sermons about love and more time loving
- Worry less about being right and more about being righteous
- Focus less on building my ministry and more on building people
- Talk less about justice and do more justice

I invite you to join me in this commitment.

The Simplicity on the Other Side

Oliver Wendell Holmes Jr. said, "I would not give a fig for the simplicity on this side of complexity, but I would give my life for the simplicity on the other side of complexity."[146]

We've journeyed through the complexity of unlimited love, systemic justice, and enduring faith. Now we arrive at the simplicity on the other side:

Love God. Love people. Do it without limits. Do it with actions. Do it until you die.

That's it. That's everything.

The Final Word

Church, the world doesn't need another book about love. It needs people who love. It doesn't need more sermons about justice. It needs people pursuing justice. It doesn't need more songs about faith. It needs people living by faith.

Be those people. Live WIDE open. Love without limits. Say less, love more.

The world is dying for lack of this kind of love. Don't let it die on your watch.

Go love like your life depends on it. Because someone's life does. Maybe even your own.

Now go and live it.

30-Day

WIDE Open Challenge

Week 1: Foundation Building

Days 1-3: Connect

- Spend 15 minutes each morning receiving God's love
- Write down one way God showed His love for you each day
- Practice saying "I am beloved" without conditions

Days 4-7: Ask

- Add midday prayer: "Lord, show me who needs love today"

- Notice three people each day who might need encouragement
- Begin seeing every encounter as a divine appointment

Week 2: Vision Development

Days 8-10: See People

- Practice the "Image of God" exercise with difficult people
- Look for one positive trait in every person you meet
- Ask yourself "What's the story behind their story?"

Days 11-14: See Systems

- Learn about one justice issue in your community
- Identify one way you benefit from current systems
- Connect with one organization working for change

Week 3: Love in Action

Days 15-17: Unlimited Love

- Remove one condition from your love for family members

- Forgive someone without them asking
- Love someone who can't reciprocate

Days 18-21: Justice Work

- Take one concrete action for justice
- Speak up about one injustice you see
- Use your resources to help one marginalized person

Week 4: Integration and Endurance

Days 22-24: Building Others

- Speak life over one person each day
- Create one opportunity for someone else to shine
- Build up someone who's different from you

Days 25-28: Staying Strong

- Practice endurance through one difficult situation
- Support someone else who's struggling
- Celebrate progress, not just perfection

Days 29-30: Full WIDE Open

- Live one complete day fully WIDE open
- Integrate all four elements: seeing, loving, justice, endurance

- Commit to continuing this lifestyle beyond 30 days

Daily CARE Practice (All 30 Days)

Morning: Connect with God's love for 5-10 minutes Midday: Ask God to show you who needs love Afternoon: Respond with one loving action Evening: Evaluate and give thanks for 5 minutes

Enhanced Bibliography

Primary Scripture References

The Holy Bible, New International Version. Biblica, 2011. The Holy Bible, New Revised Standard Version. National Council of Churches, 1989. The Holy Bible, King James Version. Cambridge Edition, 1769. The Holy Bible, New Living Translation. Tyndale House Foundation, 2015.

Contemporary Theological and Spiritual Formation

Austin, J. Kameron. Beautiful and Terrible Things: A Christian Struggle with Suffering, Grief, and Hope. Grand Rapids: Brazos Press, 2021.

Brown, Austin Channing. I'm Still Here: Black Dignity in a World Made for Whiteness. New York: Convergent Books, 2020.

Harper, Lisa Sharon. Fortune: How Race Broke My Family and the World—and How to Repair It All. Grand Rapids: Brazos Press, 2022.

Tisby, Jemar. How to Fight Racism: Courageous Christianity and the Journey Toward Racial Justice. Grand Rapids: Zondervan, 2021.

Uwan, Ekemini, et al. Truth's Table: Black Women's Musings on Life, Love, and Liberation. Grand Rapids: Brazos Press, 2022.

Classical Theological Works

Bonhoeffer, Dietrich. The Cost of Discipleship. New York: Touchstone, 1995.

Cone, James H. A Black Theology of Liberation. Maryknoll, NY: Orbis Books, 2010.

Cone, James H. The Cross and the Lynching Tree. Maryknoll, NY: Orbis Books, 2011.

Douglas, Kelly Brown. Stand Your Ground: Black Bodies and the Justice of God. Maryknoll, NY: Orbis Books, 2015.

Gutiérrez, Gustavo. A Theology of Liberation: History, Politics, and Salvation. Maryknoll, NY: Orbis Books, 1988.

King Jr. , Martin Luther. Strength to Love. Philadelphia: Fortress Press, 1981.

Nouwen, Henri J. M. The Return of the Prodigal Son: A Story of Homecoming. New York: Doubleday, 1994.

Rohr, Richard. Falling Upward: A Spirituality for the Two Halves of Life. San Francisco: Jossey-Bass, 2011.

Sobrino, Jon. Jesus the Liberator: A Historical-Theological Reading of Jesus of Nazareth. Maryknoll, NY: Orbis Books, 1993.

Thurman, Howard. Jesus and the Disinherited. Boston: Beacon Press, 1996.

Current Psychology and Neuroscience Research

Eberhardt, Jennifer. Biased: Uncovering the Hidden Prejudice That Shapes What We See, Think, and Do. New York: Penguin Books, 2020.

Gottman, John and Nan Silver. The Seven Principles for Making Marriage Work. New York: Harmony Books, 2015.

Luskin, Fred. Forgive for Good: A Proven Prescription for Health and Happiness. San Francisco: HarperOne, 2003.

Menakem, Resmaa. My Grandmother's Hands: Racialized Trauma and the Pathway to Mending Our Hearts and Bodies. Las Vegas: Central Recovery Press, 2021.

van der Kolk, Bessel. The Body Keeps the Score: Brain, Mind, and Body in the Healing of Trauma. New York: Penguin Books, 2024.

Contemporary Justice and Social Transformation

Alexander, Michelle. The New Jim Crow: Mass Incarceration in the Age of Colorblindness. New York: The New Press, 2020.

DiAngelo, Robin. Nice Racism: How Progressive White People Perpetuate Racial Harm. Boston: Beacon Press, 2021.

Hannah-Jones, Nikole. The 1619 Project: A New Origin Story. New York: One World, 2021.

Kendi, Ibram X. How to Be an Antiracist. New York: One World, 2019.

Stevenson, Bryan. Just Mercy: A Story of Justice and Redemption. New York: Spiegel & Grau, 2015.

Wilkerson, Isabel. Caste: The Origins of Our Discontents. New York: Random House, 2020.

Research and Resources (Updated 2024-2025)

HeartMath Institute. "The Science of HeartMath: Research Updates 2024." heartmath. org

The Stanford Forgiveness Project. "Longitudinal Studies on Forgiveness and Health 2020-2025." forgiveness. stanford. edu

National Institute of Mental Health. "Recent Research on Trauma, Resilience, and Community Healing." nimh. nih. gov

Equal Justice Initiative. "2024 Report on Criminal Justice Reform and Restorative Practices." eji. org

FOOTNOTES

1. For an extensive treatment of liberation theology's integration with practical spirituality, see Gustavo Gutiérrez, A Theology of Liberation: History, Politics, and Salvation (Maryknoll, NY: Orbis Books, 1988), 159-162.
2. Acts 4: 20 (NIV).
3. John 1: 39 (NIV).
4. John 20: 27 (NIV).
5. Howard Thurman, Jesus and the Disinherited (Boston: Beacon Press, 1996), 34.
6. Martin Luther King Jr. , Where Do We Go from Here: Chaos or Community? (Boston: Beacon Press, 2010), 67.
7. Galatians 5: 1 (NIV).
8. James H. Cone, A Black Theology of Liberation (Maryknoll, NY: Orbis Books, 2010), 23.
9. Amos 5: 24 (NIV).
10. ¹Isaiah 1: 17 (NIV).
11. ¹Kelly Brown Douglas, Stand Your Ground: Black Bodies and the Justice of God (Maryknoll, NY: Orbis Books, 2015), 87.
12. 1 John 4: 19 (NIV).
13. Luke 12: 7 (NIV).

14. Psalm 56: 8 (NIV).

15. Jeremiah 1: 5 (NIV).

16. Dietrich Bonhoeffer, *The Cost of Discipleship* (New York: Touchstone, 1995), 45-47.

17. John 8: 1-11 (NIV).

18. Dean Ornish, *Love and Survival: The Scientific Basis for the Healing Power of Intimacy* (New York: HarperCollins, 1998), 82.

19. The Stanford Forgiveness Project, "Research Findings on the Health Benefits of Forgiveness," Stanford University, 2000-2025, accessed January 15, 2025, forgiveness. stanford. edu.

20. Fred Luskin, *Forgive for Good: A Proven Prescription for Health and Happiness* (San Francisco: HarperOne, 2003), 45.

21. Henri J. M. Nouwen, *The Return of the Prodigal Son: A Story of Homecoming* (New York: Doubleday, 1994), 95-98.

22. Parker J. Palmer, *Let Your Life Speak: Listening for the Voice of Vocation* (San Francisco: Jossey-Bass, 2000), 44.

23. James H. Cone, *The Cross and the Lynching Tree* (Maryknoll, NY: Orbis Books, 2011), 156.

24. Gustavo Gutiérrez, *A Theology of Liberation*, 189.

25. Galatians 2: 20 (NIV).

26. Romans 8: 38-39 (NIV).

27. Richard Rohr, *Falling Upward: A Spirituality for the Two Halves of Life* (San Francisco: Jossey-Bass, 2011), 89.

28. Viktor E. Frankl, *Man's Search for Meaning* (Boston: Beacon Press, 2006), 86-87.

29. Howard Thurman, *Jesus and the Disinherited*, 98.

30. *1 Samuel 16: 7 (NIV).*

31. *Exodus 1: 16 (NIV).*

32. *Matthew 2: 16 (NIV).*

33. *James H. Cone, A Black Theology of Liberation, 134.*

34. *Genesis 37-50 (NIV).*

35. *Genesis 50: 20 (NIV).*

36. *1 Samuel 16: 11-13 (NIV).*

37. *Ezekiel 37: 1-14 (NIV).*

38. *Luke 1: 26-38 (NIV).*

39. *Martin Luther King Jr. , Strength to Love (Philadelphia: Fortress Press, 1981), 47.*

40. *John 8: 3-11 (NIV).*

41. *Mark 3: 1-6 (NIV).*

42. *Matthew 7: 3-5 (NIV).*

43. *Bryan Stevenson, Just Mercy: A Story of Justice and Redemption (New York: Spiegel & Grau, 2015), 142.*

44. *1 Corinthians 13: 12 (KJV).*

45. *John Gottman, The Seven Principles for Making Marriage Work (New York: Harmony Books, 2015), 68.*

46. *Michelle Alexander, The New Jim Crow: Mass Incarceration in the Age of Colorblindness (New York: The New Press, 2020), 95.*

47. *Kelly Brown Douglas, Stand Your Ground, 112.*

48. *Henri J. M. Nouwen, The Return of the Prodigal Son, 103.*

49. *John 4: 34 (NIV).*

50. *Luke 22: 42-44 (NIV).*

51. *Luke 22: 42 (NIV).*

52. *Jon Sobrino, Jesus the Liberator: A Historical-Theological Reading of Jesus of Nazareth (Maryknoll, NY: Orbis Books, 1993), 201.*

53. *John 5: 19 (NIV).*

54. John 5: 30 (NIV).

55. John 14: 10 (NIV).

56. Watchman Nee, Spiritual Authority (New York: Christian Fellowship Publishers, Inc. , 1972), 10-12.

57. Matthew 9: 10-13 (NIV).

58. Matthew 8: 1-4 (NIV).

59. Mark 2: 5-12 (NIV).

60. Eric Metaxas, Bonhoeffer: Pastor, Martyr, Prophet, Spy (Nashville: Thomas Nelson, 2010), 456-478.

61. Gustavo Gutiérrez, A Theology of Liberation, 287.

62. John 16: 13 (NIV).

63. Luke 5: 16 (NIV).

64. Mark 1: 35 (NIV).

65. Daniel 6 (NIV).

66. 2 Corinthians 12: 10 (NIV).

67. Matthew 5: 44 (NIV).

68. Matthew 5: 44 (NIV).

69. Matthew 18: 22 (NIV).

70. Mark 10: 21-22 (NIV).

71. John 2: 24 (NIV).

72. Luke 15: 20 (NIV).

73. HeartMath Institute, "The Science of HeartMath, " accessed January 15, 2025, heartmath. org.

74. John Gottman, The Seven Principles for Making Marriage Work, 89.

75. Martin Luther King Jr. , Strength to Love, 53.

76. James H. Cone, A Black Theology of Liberation, 178.

77. 2 Corinthians 12: 9 (NIV).

78. Romans 8: 11 (NIV).

79. 1 John 4: 18 (NIV).

80. Romans 12: 18 (NIV).

81. Acts 7: 59-60 (NIV).

82. *2 Corinthians 11: 23-28 (NIV).*

83. *Henry Cloud and John Townsend, Boundaries: When to Say Yes, How to Say No to Take Control of Your Life (Grand Rapids: Zondervan, 2017), 29-31.*

84. *Matthew 16: 23 (NIV).*

85. *Galatians 2: 11-14 (NIV).*

86. *2 Samuel 12: 1-14 (NIV).*

87. *Matthew 7: 5 (NIV).*

88. *Matthew 18: 15-17 (NIV).*

89. *Luke 13: 34 (NIV).*

90. *Luke 15: 11-32 (NIV).*

91. *Matthew 11: 30 (NIV).*

92. *Galatians 5: 1 (NIV).*

93. *John 16: 13 (NIV).*

94. *Proverbs 11: 14 (NIV).*

95. *Isaiah 58: 6-7 (NIV).*

96. *Jon Sobrino, Jesus the Liberator, 234.*

97. *Proverbs 16: 9 (NIV).*

98. *Psalm 23: 1 (NIV).*

99. *1 Thessalonians 5: 11 (NIV).*

100. *Ephesians 4: 12 (NIV).*

101. *Robert Rosenthal and Lenore Jacobson, Pygmalion in the Classroom: Teacher Expectation and Pupils' Intellectual Development (Carmarthen, Wales: Crown House Publishing, 2003), 174.*

102. *John Gottman, The Seven Principles for Making Marriage Work, 68.*

103. *Proverbs 18: 21 (NIV).*

104. *Matthew 16: 18 (NIV).*

105. *Matthew 9: 9 (NIV).*

106. *John 20: 11-18 (NIV).*

107. *Amos 5: 24 (NIV).*

108. *Exodus 34: 6-7 (NIV).*

109. *Isaiah 1: 17 (NIV).*

110. *Matthew 21: 12-13 (NIV).*

111. *Mark 12: 40 (NIV).*

112. *Luke 5: 30 (NIV).*

113. *Mark 3: 1-5 (NIV).*

114. *Luke 8: 1-3 (NIV).*

115. *Matthew 8: 3 (NIV).*

116. *Cornel West, Race Matters (Boston: Beacon Press, 2017), 15.*

117. *Matthew 5: 10 (NIV).*

118. *Stephen B. Oates, Let the Trumpet Sound: A Life of Martin Luther King, Jr. (New York: Harper Perennial, 1994), 487.*

119. *Matthew 16: 24 (NIV).*

120. *Gustavo Gutiérrez, A Theology of Liberation, 287.*

121. *James H. Cone, A Black Theology of Liberation, 112.*

122. *Jon Sobrino, Jesus the Liberator, 78.*

123. *Gustavo Gutiérrez, A Theology of Liberation, 301.*

124. *James H. Cone, The Cross and the Lynching Tree, 23.*

125. *Luke 1: 51-53 (NIV).*

126. *John 8: 1-11 (NIV).*

127. *Matthew 21: 12-13; Luke 23: 34 (NIV).*

128. *Bryan Stevenson, Just Mercy, 18.*

129. *James 1: 2-3 (NIV).*

130. *John 16: 33 (NIV).*

131. *Matthew 4: 1 (NIV).*

132. *Howard Thurman, Jesus and the Disinherited, 45.*

133. *Jeremiah 17: 7-8 (NIV).*

134. *Viktor E. Frankl, Man's Search for Meaning, 126.*

135. *Ecclesiastes 4: 12 (NIV).*

136. *Matthew 11: 3 (NIV).*

173

137. *Matthew 26: 38 (NIV).*
138. *1 Corinthians 6: 19 (NIV).*
139. *John 10: 10 (NIV).*
140. *1 John 4: 18 (NIV).*
141. *2 Timothy 1: 7 (NIV).*
142. *Romans 12: 2 (NIV).*
143. *John 10: 10 (NIV).*
144. *1 John 3: 18 (NIV).*
145. *James 1: 22 (NIV).*
146. *Oliver Wendell Holmes Jr. , quoted in multiple sources, original letter to Art Young, 1935.*